The Relationship Handbook

The Relationship Handbook

Jan S. Maizler

Writers Club Press
New York Lincoln Shanghai

The Relationship Handbook

Writers Club Press
an imprint of iUniverse, Inc.

For information address:
iUniverse, Inc.
2021 Pine Lake Road, Suite 100
Lincoln, NE 68512
www.iuniverse.com

ISBN: 0-595-25912-X (pbk)

ISBN: 0-595-65427-4 (cloth)

Printed in the United States of America

Contents

Foreword

It is a sad yet curious fact that North American and European society have basically no academic learning and training in relationship health. Physical education and fitness have been given far more attention: while it is good to be trained in this area, it is crucial to devote the same academic energy to relationships.

The building block of our society is the family and the core of the family is inevitably a relationship: parent to child, parent to parent, or partner to partner. The family—in its many modern forms—is also the hatching ground for every individual life. It is commonly acknowledged that good mental health of a child is more likely when they come from functional families (versus dysfunctional families.)

From their own academic training, parents teach their children not to smoke, and to do pushups and eat their vegetables. But they have no scientific information about relationships that they can pass on to their children. In turn, their children grow up and form their own relationships, generally (yet unconsciously) relying on the foggy, unmindful relations they absorbed from their own family of origin.

This book is devoted to your conscious, mindful education about deep intimate relationships that appear in healthy couples, marriages, and families. It is written and designed as an "interactive" educational book that will be used repeatedly as a resource. Because the goal of this book is to teach, certain key concepts are repeated because their importance warrants it.

Jan Maizler
Miami, Florida 2002

Contributors

Sandy Allen is the editor of *The Relationship Handbook*. She can be reached at **sandraalleninc@mindspring.com** or (305) 274-4613.

Shermin Davis is the project administrator of *The Relationship Handbook*. Visit her website at **www.humane-resources.com**. She is in private practice as a coach, counselor, and case manager.

1

Readiness for Relationships
(Stage 1)

A relationship is any arrangement between two people where the terms of that arrangement are generally understood. This book explores relationships of deep friendship or love that require considerable emotional investment or intimacy.

An individual's intrapersonal development is an important prelude to optimal functioning in a relationship with another person. Successful completion of this "inner work" helps to provide personal stability. Personal stability raises our level of readiness for forging new relationships.

Three basic elements of this inner work are a sense of completeness, fulfillment of potential, and the ability (and action) to take care of ourselves.

Sense of Completeness

At some point in their lives, most people achieve a state of development where they feel relatively complete. This process starts in childhood and continues through adult life. Without this sense of completeness, a person has "gaps" that need to be filled. If an individual enters into a relationship before they have developed this sense of completeness, they will inevitably use the other person to fill their own gaps. Instead of creating a healthy relationship, they develop a sense of dependency toward the other person.

When each individual completes their inner work prior to forging a relationship, they come together with a healthy sense of individuality and can better focus on developing a healthy relationship.

Fulfillment of Potential

All people are born with gifts and aptitudes. Most of us use these gifts and aptitudes to do positive things that contribute to the good of our families, communities, and our world. Many of us acquire and develop additional skills along the way. We desire to feel good, skilled, excellent, and competent at things. We want to feel as though we matter—as though we help the world in some way. Our gifts, aptitudes, and skills are vehicles of addressing these important needs.

A person who feels that they have not fully blossomed in their potential abilities will always feel a sense of frustration, sadness, and disappointment.

Ability to Take Care of Ourselves

Childhood and adolescence is the training period for us, as individuals, to learn the skills necessary to take care of ourselves in our adult lives. We must learn how to take care of our physical and emotional needs in order to survive, but most of us want to accomplish much more than just survival.

Parents provide the teaching and emotional support to help their children develop survival skills to deal with frustration, acquire a sense of achievement, and enhance their physical and emotional development. Parents who coddle and overindulge their children, and do not allow them to do what they can and should do for themselves, create feelings of helplessness in the child. This behavior is known as "enabling" and usually results in chronic morbid dependency.

Anyone that still suffers from morbid dependency will enter a relationship as a "Tower of Pisa"—their wish to lean on their partner will be prominent. The other person will feel the weight and strain of their partner's leaning and will usually grow tired of this arrangement.

While survival can be accomplished with a minimal level of skill, our desire to achieve a sense of completeness, to reach our maximum potential and to take care of ourselves are internal stimuli that motivate us to take on the task of our inner work.

A healthy functional relationship is comprised of two partners that have largely completed their intrapersonal, prerelationship inner work.

Where are you in the process of completing your "inner work"?

List the ways that you feel or don't feel complete:

   Complete:

   Incomplete:

List the ways you feel that you have or have not reached your potential:

   Reached:

   Have not reached:

List the ways you feel you are able or not able to take care of yourself:

   Able:

   Not able:

2

Relationships and the Interpersonal World (Stage 2)

We do not have to engage the interpersonal world. We can continue to garden, cultivate, and to harvest our inner world. But an intimate relationship has the potential to bear fruits that a life of solitude cannot.

Our relations with others bring lessons and growth opportunities. We need to have other people in our lives so that we can keep tabs on our own interpersonal behavior. Repeated exposure to others allows us to recognize repeating patterns of successful or impaired relations. Recognizing our own patterns of behavior helps us determine which behaviors are positive and which behaviors should be modified. Through observation, ownership, appraisal, and management, we are able to complete the cycle of transformation and grow deeper in our emotional bonding in a relationship.

Cathexis

Cathexis is the presence and extent of emotional investment in a relationship. Cathexis determines the depth of the relationship for each person. Whether it is a loving, fighting, or tidal (on-and-off) relationship, the level of cathexis determines how much effort and energy an individual will exert to keep the relationship going.

Relationships

Relationships are either functional, dysfunctional, or somewhere in between. What distinguishes a functional relationship is that it carries forward the work done individually (in prerelationship) and allows two individuals to explore the challenges, develop the skills, and share the benefits created by the evolving relationship. Intimacy is perhaps the greatest benefit of a functional relationship. Intimacy is a progressive process of a knowing, sharing, and disclosing closeness.

Dysfunctional relationships, on the other hand, do not extend prerelationship work. Rather than a nurturing of each other's individual selves, there is a sense of fear, turmoil, and isolation.

3

Creating and Maintaining a Healthy, Functional Relationship (Stage 3)

The three main elements of a healthy relationship are a gratifying interpersonal mix, the esteeming of the other partner through word and action, and the maintenance of mutual emotional safety through commitment.

A Gratifying Interpersonal Mix

The interplay between two people in a relationship is determined in part by compatibility. Compatibility includes a shared value system between the parties. Compatibility is often associated with longevity in relationships, in part because the pleasure associated with being alike is self-perpetuating.

Part of a gratifying interpersonal mix is what is commonly known as chemistry. This term (although not very specific) includes feelings of mutual pleasure; not just because of compatibility, but because of physical attraction, admiration of the other, and anticipated pleasure based on potential interplay.

A good mix can also be based on contrasts between the two partners. A passive partner may choose a partner with the ability to be aggressive. Not only does this create more behavioral possibilities for the new relationship, it also provides a role model of new behavior for the passive partner, which can lead to transformation. Again, there must be some degree of compatibility that gives the relationship times of pleasure, mutuality, and "rest" from interpersonal challenges. It can't always be "work."

A good mix is essential to a relationship because it provides "color," inspiration, and passion. In love relationships, both partners can create emotional safety through commitment, and can esteem each other, but the richness of the relationship depends on the mix of characteristics that the individual partners bring to the relationship.

Esteeming the Other Partner Through Word and Action

Two very strong human needs are the need to be loved by another and the need for the esteem and admiration of another. These needs continue throughout the life cycle and can manifest particularly in deep relationships where the staging ground for fulfillment of these needs is present.

Relationships are kept strong, intact, and viable by showing the other person in the relationship, by word or through action, that they are valuable and important. While a good mix may simply be the positive energy generated by what each person brings to the relationship, esteeming is a behavioral choice that is dependent on the will, motivation, and action of the individual.

Emotional Safety Through Commitment

The last element of a healthy relationship, commitment, is also a behavioral choice. Commitment in a relationship is ensured by consistent, predictable, reliable, trust-building loyalty to the relationship. It often entails making the other person in the relationship a priority. It is this repeated behavior that builds trust and emotional safety.

Emotional safety is essential to the longevity of a relationship. A love affair may begin with a passionate mix and valuing of the partner may add fuel, but lack of commitment will shorten its' life and stability significantly.

Emotional safety is essential in relationship intimacy. How willing can a person be to embrace progressive closeness if they don't feel safe with the other person in the relationship?

Does your relationship have a gratifying interpersonal mix?

Are you and your partner committed to esteeming each other through word and action?

If not, what can you do to make your partner feel valued? What do you expect your partner to do for you?

Commitment in a relationship is ensured by consistent, predictable, reliable, trust-building loyalty to the relationship.

Do you trust your partner?

Does he or she trust you?

What can you do to create or enhance trust?

What do you expect from your partner?

4

The Development of a Love Relationship

The search for a mate begins with the display of one's "plumage" and the necessity of putting one's best foot forward to attract a mate. How, when, and where the search for a mate occurs is based on the person's personality and preferences.

The Prospective Partner is Seen and Chosen

The initial basis of choosing a potential partner is their visible attributes and behavior. This includes their physical appearance, mood, and other superficial behavior. This is accomplished by looking at and observing the other person. Mutual observation and eye contact may usher in courtship if each party is pleased or curious about what they see.

Courtship and Wooing Begin

Courtship and wooing mark the first immediate interpersonal verbal contact based on mutual attraction, curiosity, and the wish for fulfillment of personal needs and drives. Each partner begins a fuller assessment of the other person's attributes, strengths, weaknesses, and general overall status in their group. This includes assessing them as a potential mate and is based on getting more information about the other person by looking at them and by talking to them.

Romance

If the wooing is mutually satisfying, each partner enters into romance with inner dreams they hope to have fulfilled. At this point, they have little information about the other, but still may see them as potential dream-fulfillers. There is no strong factual foundation at this point in the relationship.

The pleasures associated with newness gives a positive aura to the early interactions and fuel the positive projections each partner places on the other. The adventures that accompany this phase also create a sense of intoxication.

Mating

Mating is the physical or sexual aspect of the new relationship. It is one of the first challenges of the relationship as to whether there is physical harmony and compatibility between the partners. Mating also provides physical and sexual information about the other. Positive mating experiences give rise to "pairing" together.

Information

Information creates new interpersonal realities as the relationship proceeds. As information about the other unfolds, there will be an inevitable discrepancy between the hoped-for behavior of the other and their actual behavior. Time spent together as a "pair" will reveal assets and liabilities in each person. One potential emotional reaction to the possible discrepancy between inner dreams and newly revealed actual behavior is disappointment. The mythology of romanticism disrupts unfolding relationships in indicating that such disappointment is an aberration and a negative development. It tells us that pairs or couples are to only experience bliss. This fuels an early ending of relationships where romantically deluded partners part company and resume their search for their soul mate.

Romanticism actually kills the early sense of romance by insisting on a mythology of total intensity, bliss, and compatibility. In love relationships, nothing could be further from the truth. The most realistic response to the flow of new information that is disappointing is to be thoughtful and reflective of what this means to the compatibility of the couple. Lack of compatibility usually prevents the two individuals from moving on to pairing and bonding.

Pairing and Bonding

If the information that unfolds is positive and creates comfort and compatibility for each partner, the couple moves from pairing to bonding. Bonding creates a stronger unit of relationship that has a life of its own. The partners often refer to it as "our relationship."

If the relationship has significant value for each partner, commitments to each other and to the relationship may be made to further solidify the bonding to each partner. Commitment to the relationship may not only take the form of self-sacrifice; it may also mean making your relationship with that person the primary focus in your life.

The Couple, the Passage of Time, and Change

The passage of time brings inevitable change for couples. Not only does new information continue to flow about the partner, but also the inevitable challenges of life visit the couple. The relationship must process new experiences and new information in order to survive.

As the couple moves along, the inevitable needs discrepancies that two separate people have make needs negotiations necessary. This phase of relationship relies heavily on healthy relationship skills for its ongoing development and evolution.

Less mature individuals or those who have not completed their inner work may end a relationship once the intoxication of romance is replaced by the challenges of new information. Others may reach some level of bonding, but lack the relationship skills to effectively function as a healthy pair as the couple proceeds through time and change. For example, narcissistic or self-centered individuals may be unable to weather necessary moments of self-sacrifice for their partner.

Couplehood

As couples spend more time together, a special bond develops. Partners become increasingly invested in each other and begin to place more and more value on their investment. In addition to the length of time partners spend together, the information they accrue about each other adds value to the relationship. They grow accustomed to the comfortable and predictable familiarity of each other.

Generally, the mysteries, fantasies, and projections have evaporated in healthier partners capable of living in the present moment. What replaces them is a predictable body of knowledge of the pros and cons of the significant other.

If the assets exceed the liabilities and the relationship is not dysfunctional, a growing acceptance of the "now real" partner occurs. Psychologically mature partners can accept and bear their ambivalence towards their partner in realizing that there is much to like and dislike in the very same person. These challenges will help give rise to newer tools acquired and utilized in an atmosphere of increased closeness and intimacy. This closeness builds on itself, as each partner is witness to their partner's struggles and growth.

Growth and Interdependence

The mature phases of the life of a functional relationship are highlighted by many of the following characteristics:

- Willingness and commitment to adapt to the changes that inevitably accompany a long time spent together.
- The relationship takes on a "life of its own."

- Each person is now real, with full information "display." The factual foundation for the couple is strong.

- Needs negotiation and other relationship skills are utilized and enhanced over time.

- Discomforts in the relationship are not seen as loss of love, but as growth opportunities. Further time spent together lends itself to a refocusing to the psychological, interior forces of the couple as opposed to the early assessment of physical attraction and unfulfilled needs. The mature couple can grow interdependently and individually as well.

If you are in a developing love relationship, what stage do you think it is in?

5

Romanticism versus Relationship Realism

One of the central concepts you will find repeatedly in this book is that romanticism is the bane of healthy functional relationships.

Romanticism is based on myths and wishes. Relationship realism is based on scientific information and effective technique.

One compelling relationship issue is the concept of lifetime pairing. In our society, long-lived marriages are encouraged, celebrated, and reinforced. Twenty-five years of marriage is given silver status, and fifty years of marriage is given gold status. The longer the marriage lasts, the more noble the metal it becomes: this is the romantic part.

The factual part of lifetime pairing is that sanctioning of longer-lasting families may have a stabilizing effect on society, in that the offspring of still-married families are more "settled." Although this may be a possibility, recent trends in relationship demography indicate this consideration is not enough to stay "paired" at all costs.

Indeed, lifetime pairing is sometimes harmful and unwise for all the parties involved. "Going the distance" just to get the silver or gold may not be worth the price of the suffering.

Before the idea of lifetime couplehood is even contemplated, relationship realism pays attention to and embraces facts and information, not fantasy. The following ideas will be repeated because of their importance:

- Relationships and the people that comprise them will initiate and/or experience change. This is inevitable.

- Relationships are like gardens. They will grow in one set of conditions and die under another set. Relationships are not unconditional.

- Relationships, like a garden, take work. If you think this is too much work, maybe you are not ready.

- The end of mystique-based novelty and newness in all our relationships is a certainty.

- The intoxication of newness is going to be effected by the law of diminishing returns.

- All new relationships are pulled together through courtships. This entails attracting a partner through the display of puffed up plumage and other displays of visible and tangible attractants. *Courtship in nature is temporary—it is designed to begin a relationship, not maintain it.*

- When the people "couple," courtship ceases, romance runs its course, and facts make their appearance. This may be a loss to the couple, as the assumption that courtship plumage was a permanent state is shattered.

As couples learn the actual unfolding facts about each other—each person's assets and liabilities—an overall tangible outline of each other is formed.

Romanticism has often cast its black magic in the area as well, in some way negatively conveying that there is nothing "new" to discover. The relationships realist celebrates the arrival of this state in that a more complete "informational layout" gives you the basis for the best management of your relationship.

The loss of "newness" can be replaced with the advent of new inner skills in each partner. This is cultivated by tolerating the loss of courtship romance and "working the informational layout" with ever-increasing effectiveness. An example of this would be an enhanced ability to respond to your partner's character defects and imperfections with increasing patience.

The state of "singlehood" offers little opportunity to grow in so many ways. One's defects need not ever go challenged in this kingdom of one. People cannot often see themselves accurately. Long-time single people grow accustomed to themselves as they are and are not challenged to face compromise, uncomfortable observations, and growth-inducing conflicts that a relationship would bring. A single person who lives alone can say and do whatever they please in their own presence.

People in relationships are so very fortunate in that they have the opportunity to learn, effectively cultivate, and finally internalize the need for self-control. In the society of a relationship, the growth of self-control in one's words or actions becomes an enormously effective tool in reducing conflict and maintaining stability in the relationship and in the world beyond the relationship. The single person living alone does not have the benefit of such a daily, on-site opportunity.

A relationship offers certain opportunities for growth, change, and transformation that a single life cannot.

Realistic couples brave the departure and loss of romantic newness and experience the emergence of a new relationship trend: the couple slowly becomes a "we" which means a unit that takes on a life of its own and generates a microculture and life that is utterly unique and never to be repeated again, anytime, anywhere. The growth of "we" in a couple is particularly enhanced and given nourishment for a long journey through space and time if the partners in the relationship are highly compatible. The "we" feeling will help the couple manage the reality that:

- Feelings in relationships can change;

- People in relationships can and do make choices that will impact and change the status quo "steady state" of the relationship; and

- Adjustments and change will be needed to create a "new" steady state.

6

The Myths that Delude Couples

Romanticism is a powerful adversary for relationship realism. It has roots that extend deep into history and it crosses into many societies. Relationship romanticism is founded upon and has spawned many myths and fairy tales. More prominent among them are:

- "Someday my prince will come" portrays a magical rescue by a perfect man that will lift the woman out of her struggles and up into love rapture.

- "The soul mate" conveys the idea that a perfect match is "out there" waiting for you. This person will bring the relationship eternal happiness.

- 'Til death do us part" is a belief that relationships are sanctified only by a lifetime oath and commitment. Any variable that might change this oath goes unexamined.

- "Someone who has been married many times is a neurotic failure." If you have had an "infinite" or prodigiously long string of unmarried relationships, you are seen as popular, strong, and experienced. The label of neuroticism seems to be kept locked up until you marry.

- "Let's see what happens (in the relationship)." Relationships, of course, do not "happen" any more than a garden "happens." If a garden has weeds, they need plucking. A relationship that is not modified will remain the same.

- "Let's give the relationship some space." Exactly what distancing each other is supposed to accomplish remains unclear. If the couple parts, perhaps they will find out they will miss each other, and to diminish the pain of loneliness and longing, the couple may recombine. Of course, the conditions that caused them to take space will reactivate as soon as the residual pain of the parting diminishes.

- "A relationship or marriage can make a good man or woman out of you." There is no basis for this myth any more than planting a weed in a garden will turn it into a rose. Therapists work with a psychological truth that asserts, "wherever you go, there you are!" The fact is that people change themselves from within. A relationship can challenge someone to change, but the relationship itself cannot bestow change.

- "When the thrill is gone, there's something wrong with the relationship." The fact is, when the thrill is gone is when the real relationship begins.

- "When the thrill is gone, it's time for you to move on" is another crazy-making myth. When the thrill is gone and you want to move on, it's time for you to get treatment.

- "A good relationship should be able to endure anything." Any relationship that endures everything desperately needs treatment.

- "No one really understands love." This is romanticism's most poisonous myth and dooms otherwise thoughtful people to endless wandering around in the dark. Love is understandable and manageable.

List any romantic myths that have affected you or are still affecting you.

7

The Foundations of Relationship Realism

Relationship realism is founded on personal retraining, insight aimed at accurate information (facts), and a commitment to ongoing and conscious maintenance.

Personal Retraining

As stated in the foreword, there is no automatic formal academic training in relationships. Sex education, personal hygiene, and physical fitness receive the attention they need in our schools, but nothing is taught about the skills (or lack of skills) that will form the core of every family. Therefore, it is inevitable that the vast majority of Americans will carry inside them the untrained and inevitably, dysfunctional software they have downloaded from viewing their parents' or caregivers' relationships. So, if your mom married, suffered with, and stuck it out with your alcoholic dad, that is the software you start with. Day after day as a child, you lived with an illness that was part of everyday life. To others, it would seem horrible; to you, it became normative. It would be no surprise if you found yourself attracted to, overly tolerant of, or vehemently despising your partner if they were alcoholic: all three of these variations mean you're still running the same dysfunctional software.

Personal retraining is based on the understanding gained in doing the personal work necessary to be aware of your situation and change it. (This may involve therapy, workshops, meetings, seminars, etc.) If you are in an unhappy, crazy relationship, you must be doing something very wrong.

Personal retraining, then, means fixing yourself so you become healthy. Healthy people make healthy choices and healthy relationships are comprised of healthy people.

Do you feel you need personal retraining?

If so, list the ways you can accomplish this.

Insight Aimed at Accurate Information

Another foundation of relationship realism is based on the maxim, "choose your partner based on who they really are, rather than your 'idea' of them." Success in a relationship depends on a clear appraisal of your significant other. Do not make them one of your inner cast of characters in your unresolved conflicts. Face up to newly discovered problems like addiction, mental illness, or unresolved baggage in yourself or your significant other.

Learn as much as possible about your potential partner by investigating the facts:

- Find out all you can about their family of origin, particularly the assets and liabilities of their parents.

- Find out all you can about what happened to them in their family of origin.

- Find out what they've learned about themselves from their past relationships.

- If given the opportunity, be willing to hear about them from their family members, children, ex-spouses, etc.

- Find out their basic belief or beliefs about life itself.

- Appraise the data you have collected to see if it yields compatibility (versus incompatibility) with you.

Obviously, this will take time, but the information it yields can make the difference between a life of joy and a life of suffering. If you were thinking of hiring a person in business, you would ask for a resume and references: should a relationship deserve less? Consider the following:

- The most potent and accurate information about an individual does not present itself until after the courtship behavior ends and until your (romanticized and idealized) idea of the person is tested for accuracy by spending time with this person.

- The time spent learning about the other person should be long and thorough enough to give reliable information. Consider the benefits of living together prior to marriage.

- It may be wise to experience sex prior to making any serious commitment; it is risky to not experience and assess something so important before the marital commitment commences. This is the reason people "test drive" a car—although the comparison is crude, the parallel still holds.

- Spend enough time together so that the software each partner has downloaded from his or her parents is activated in the face of impending commitment. Far too often, this downloaded software remains dormant in casual flings and romances. People who are not conscious of their downloads and have not retrained themselves will begin to duplicate their parents behavior as the relationship goes on.

- A "light-to-heavy" scale is an interpersonality tool that can help you and your partner evaluate your compatibility.

The "light-to-heavy" scale assesses relationships from the perspective of "interpersonal weight." At one extreme of the scale, "light people" are characterized by, and emphasize logic, intellect, non-emotionalism, non-confrontation, and concern over the impact of their actions on others. They emphasize inner processes and inner resolutions. They have a low interpersonal impact on a relationship. "Heavy people," on the other hand, tend to emphasize feelings over intellect and logic. They are comfortable being deep in their feelings and "working them." Because of the primacy of their feelings and the need to process them, there is far less concern about confrontations between people because they see it as a necessary step towards resolution. Additionally, therefore, their emotive processing would also place far less concern on their impact on others. ("Send the steak back if you don't like it! Who cares if the waiter said it was the house specialty?") Heavy people place more emphasis on interpersonal processes and resolutions. Issues and conflicts are necessary and require immediate discussion, processing, and resolution. Obviously, "heavy people" bring a strong interpersonal impact to a relationship. Although the "light-to-heavy" scale is somewhat arbitrary, it has its utility in the most tangible ways.

One newly married couple had to deal with the wife's ex-husband because of their eight-year-old daughter conceived in the prior marriage. The ex-husband's behavior was appalling: no-shows on visitation days, late or insufficient child support payments, and general irresponsibility when vacation planning was attempted. The new husband was the "heavy" one. He wanted to confront the ex-husband. He saw his stepdaughter's disappointment, and the painful letdowns were ample reason to "put the coals" to the ex-husband. He felt any confrontations, including legal action, were unavoidably necessary and important steps to resolving the problems caused by the ex-husband. The wife was the "light" one in the new marriage. She wanted as little to do with the ex-husband as possible—had she not divorced him for this very reason? She saw confrontation with the ex-husband as undesirable because it re-invoked the same poison she had left. She felt that any confrontation between the new marriage and the ex-husband was giving the ex-husband "too much power" in the new marriage. "Why bother thinking about him…that's the way he is. No-shows and short support payments are what he's all about." She also felt that increased confrontation and conflict amongst the new marriage and the ex-husband could generate enough discomfort in the latter that he would withdraw entirely from his young daughter or that the conflict would be felt by the daughter herself and damage her emotionally in some way.

Clearly, in the above vignette, neither party is right or wrong. They both have cogent points that are valid. The point here is that their non-compatibility on the light-to-heavy scale caused considerable and prolonged painful conflict between them in this and many, many other situations.

As an epilogue, their profound incompatibility on the "light-to-heavy" scale did take a toll on the relationship. He, over time, increasingly saw his wife as avoidant, expedient, unprincipled, codependent, and afraid. On her part, she increasingly saw her husband as judgmental, an embarrassment, a bellicose warrior, and angry. Their "styles" were so divergent and incompatible that what little satisfaction they had dwindled and they grew apart over the different ways they handled life. They eventually divorced. Hopefully, they found more compatible partners.

If partners have mild contrasts on the "light-to-heavy" scale, there is enough common ground to bear their differences. In fact, in this scenario there is much they can teach each other.

Describe what you have done to learn about your potential partners.

Ongoing and Conscious Maintenance

This is the long-term working tool of relationship realism. It is predicated on two scientific truths about you and your relationships. First, you must commit yourself to the belief that relationships require ongoing maintenance to be healthy and sound. Second, you must commit yourself to the belief that maintenance is most effective when it is "conscious." This means having the fullest knowledge and awareness of feelings and dynamics occurring between you and your partner. This includes accepting that, as people, you and your partner have intricate, complex, and multi-layered feelings. These feelings can be uncomfortable and they can be unconscious. They can also be ambivalent which might even mean acknowledging being angry and hateful at your partner, yet loving them at the same time.

Rather than wilting when anger appears in a love relationship, relationship realism accepts that this need not be alarming or problematic. However, if anger in a relationship becomes persistent, prodigious and chronic, relationship realism endorses and insists that this has now become a problem that warrants attention and resolution. This kind of relationship maintenance is known as conflict resolution.

The five steps of conflict resolution in a healthy, ongoing relationship consist of: common acknowledgement, self-ownership of misbehavior, empathic acknowledgment or mirroring, amends-making, and ongoing behavioral modification.

Common Acknowledgement. Mutual acknowledgement indicates that both parties are conscious of a specific problem that exists between them that needs resolution.

Self-ownership of the Misbehavior. Although nothing happens in isolation, one person may be largely responsible for initiating a problem (for example, habitually criticizing or devaluing their partner publicly). In this case, the initial task is a dialogue between the partners about the devaluing behavior and dispassionately going over the origin of the behavior. If the initiating partner is non-defensive, unemotional, and courageous, he or she will claim ownership. This is a positive development, because claiming ownership of misbehavior builds trust and role models similar behavior for the other partner. It also gives considerable power to the "owner" of the misbehavior because claiming something creates more control in changing it.

Empathic Acknowledgement or Mirroring. The next step of conscious conflict resolution should be to attempt to feel as fully as possible what the other person feels in the conflict. For example, the partner (who embarrassed the second party) might try to deeply imagine what they feel and state, "you must have felt so embarrassed, humiliated, and diminished by what I said to you. That must have been awful."

Amends-Making. There is room in amends-making for "I am so sorry." That is an acknowledgement of personal distress, remorse, guilt, and deep concern over the pain created in your partner by your behavior. Amends-making is a moral step that indicates not only responsibility for one's misbehavior, but an anguished and committed intention to stop that misbehavior. Ongoing amends-making over the same repeating misbehavior reveals this to be only an empty device that plays a role in the problem staying alive and unfixed.

Ongoing Behavioral Modification. The final step of conflict resolution is ongoing behavior modification. Although the fuel and source of behavioral changes may be couple's dialogue, self-help, group help, seminars, workshops, or professional help, the person seeking change must change themselves. In the final analysis, they are on their own and can expect that the modification of their behavior will and can be quite uncomfortable. Something that will "balance" and put this discomfort in perspective is that living life in the sick way they have is no longer an alternative. This is known as "surrender" and can make change and its discomfort easier. This final step is when the seeker of behavioral change employs whatever methods are necessary to modify what they have been doing in creating and prolonging the problem.

For instance, a severely compulsive overeater may have reached the point that by their forties, not only are they morbidly obese, they also may have all the diseases associated with the condition, such as hypertension, diabetes, heart disease, high blood fats, and the hip and spinal problems that come from carrying abnormally heavy weights. This person is not only risking their life by not addressing their illness; they are creating pain, distress, and suffering in their loved ones. Their "misbehavior" is causing conflict to the relative peace that would be felt if the compulsive overeating would be modified into normal eating and normal lifestyle.

List your thoughts about your efforts to provide ongoing and conscious maintenance to your relationship.

8

A Toolkit for Conflict Prevention

The following "tools" will help you avoid or resolve conflicts in all of your relationships.

Pick Your Battles

Do not get stuck into the momentary, transient conflicts that may arise from tiredness, hunger, and crankiness that will inevitably dissipate if left alone. It is only necessary to deal with real problems.

Create the Peace First

The quickest way to stop toxic conflict—such as bickering and escalation—is to stop your involvement. Simply state your wish to stop something that is becoming harmful, take a rain check, and take a time-out (or a walk). It takes two people to have conflict. Set the stage for conflict resolution (through dialogue and other means) instead of toxic conflict. Be sure to let your partner know what you see as a tangible problem and make an appointment within the next few hours to discuss it again.

Cultivate Golden Silence

It is often wise in toxic conflicts to remain silent. This is not the type of silence that conveys withdrawal, hostility, or uncommunicativeness. Golden silence is useful to stop bickering, escalation, reactivity, and litigating. It can also set the tone that if you keep eye contact with your partner—in good faith—that you will listen but not get engaged in a war of words.

Recognize You are Powerless over Others

You cannot change someone else. You cannot control someone else. And above all, you cannot make someone else feel the way you want them to: they must do that for themselves. Accepting this truth will ultimately give you great relief and great serenity. If your partner is actively addicted to gambling, and if they do not want to change this, you are powerless to do anything about it.

You Have Total Power and Control over Your Reactions

You can detach with love and leave any situation where you are being hurt. In any situation, wherever you go, you have total freedom and choice over your actions and reactions. Many people find many excuses to avoid this great truth. They blame their misfortunes. They blame their parents. They blame their childhood. They blame their spouses. They blame their emotional symptoms. Nevertheless, at all times, you have complete freedom over your reactions in the final sense.

People Always Wind up Doing What They Want to Do

Effective conflict prevention and relationship management is enhanced by realizing the enormous role that motivation plays in human relations. When someone tells you "I can't" or "I am not able to," they are ultimately saying, "I do not want to." If someone forgets something that they were supposed to do that involved you, rest assured that whatever it was, it was not in the forefront of their mind.

When Someone Else Truly has the Problem, Leave it There!

People suffering from codependency have great difficulty using this tool. Taking on another person's problems is dangerous in many ways:

- It clouds up the responsibility and necessity the other person has in changing themselves.

- The shared suffering this creates robs the "problem" person of the pain and discomfort that motivates them to change. This shared suffering then becomes the life of the couple or relationship: it becomes a life of sickness.

- It adds to the overall difficulty of living for the person taking on another's problem.

- Taking on another's problems also can grow into a devious excuse for neglecting and not taking care of yourself. If another person asks you in any way to take on their problem or to fix it, just say no!

If You Want Something From Someone Else, You Must Ask For It

It is amazing how many adults retain magical childish ideas: they still want their minds to be "read" without having to say a word. Romanticism further pollutes relationship health with such ideas as, "he completes my sentences," I never have to ask," or "she reads my mind." These ideas create confusion.

In a healthy relationship, interpersonal needs are verbalized because verbal communication is the most effective way to indicate if you want something. The best way to ask is to make a request. For instance, you could say, "If you're going to the market, I would like to go with you," or, "on my birthday, I would really appreciate a ring, necklace, wallet, etc." All your requests will not be met, but you still must ask for something if you want it.

Always Resist Reactivity

Reactivity in yourself or your partner is to be avoided. Reactivity is the fuel of runaway fights and arguments. Reactivity often stems from primordial reflexes when evolved thought and dialogue did not exist. Reactivity is the enemy of effective communication and needs negotiation. Reactivity is equated with poor impulse control.

Reactivity may manifest in a relationship that has a contentious or cranky moment, as in a tit-for-a-tat: at these times, keep yourself in check. Reactivity could also occur in this scenario: you and your partner have just returned from a jog or workout. As your partner opens the refrigerator door, you grab the water bottle and start guzzling. Ask yourself, how does this make your partner feel? In another scenario, your partner tells an embarrassing story about you in public. Your first reaction might be to recount a tale that is equally embarrassing to your partner. Ask yourself, would this accomplish anything productive?

Reactivity is primitive. Dialogue is evolved.

Compromise, Compromise, Compromise

If you break down the word compromise, you can find two key elements: "co" and "promise." For the purposes of relationship maintenance and conflict resolution, co means mutuality (a joint enterprise) and promise means a "binding," intentful pact. This is helpful in understanding that this valuable word means so much more than "giving in." Compromise in a relationship should be thought of somewhere on the level of prayer, in terms of its importance, sacredness, and utility.

Effective compromise is an extremely potent tool in relationships. Compromise is achieved via dialogue, needs negotiation, and some personal "stretching" into discomfort: this entails the same gestures for each partner. It is based on the thinking that a little mutual "stretching" of each partner will result in gratification for both. For instance,

Bill and Kathy were vacationing in the American Southwest. After they arrived, unpacked, and got "situated," it was late afternoon. Bill wanted to go hiking in the hills surrounding the town, and catch the upcoming sunset. Kathy wanted to catch the remaining open hours of some of the local art galleries. Both verbalized their needs, which turned out not to be the same. There were various alternatives. They could each pursue their own needs and meet up later, but that would mean the loss of one another's company and fellowship from the start of their vacation. They discussed this and ruled it out. Bill suggested that he would go with Kathy to the shops and perhaps they could get up early the next morning and catch the sunrise in these same hills. This was acceptable to her, even though she might have to get up earlier than she wanted for the next day. The couple had achieved a successful compromise. Each partner was willing to diminish their needs gratification a bit to satisfy their partner for the good of the relationship.

Compromise is a tool that can cope with minor conflicts that could conceivably become major flare-ups. Roberta loved to sleep with the air conditioner quite cold. Her partner, Peter, liked it rather warm. In order to sleep together in relative comfort, she agreed to make the temperature a bit warmer. He agreed to wear heavier pajamas to bed and cope with the air conditioner being a bit cooler than was ideal for him. The compromise of one partner shows the other partner that they are important and the relationship is important enough that each party is willing to "roll back" their needs.

Avoid Arguing at all Costs

One of the strongest pillars of a healthy relationship rests on the idea that arguments poison a relationship and dialogue strengthens it. During an argument, all hearing and listening come to an end. During an argument, communication dies. During an argument, abuse and physical violence remain an ever-present possibility. During an argument, primitive behaviors are unleashed that include verbal growling, malice, aggression, and destructive verbal (name calling) and nonverbal (face-offs) behaviors. This can cause emotional damage. Both partners regress, injure one another, and cause scars. Although the argument may subside quickly, no amount of apology or rationalization can really heal the damage done: words said during the heat of argument still hurt and words carry as much destructive power as sticks and stones.

More importantly, arguments and the damage they cause become a part of the life and history of the relationship. History cannot be rewritten. A garden assaulted repeatedly by the vermin, droughts, and sunless days of fighting, mean-spiritedness, and damaging aggressiveness will eventually die.

Engage in Effective Dialogue

Effective dialogue is predicated on appropriate listening and appropriate speaking.

"Good (appropriate) listening" involves really hearing your partner. Your head must be clear and free of thoughts. You must be in a state of reception. If you are merely waiting for your partner to be done speaking so you can "have your say," you are certainly not listening.

A maxim of a good dialogue is that you cannot listen if you are speaking. In treatment, I counsel all my couples that one person must choose to be the speaker, and the other person will be the listener. Then the process will be reversed.

It has been my experience as a clinician that listening can have more power than speaking at times. Listening to the speaker gives them the room and freedom to express, explore, integrate, and heal "on their own." Listening also empowers the listener's focus, sensitivity, and mental clarity.

"Good (appropriate) speaking" is based on the provision of information by the speaker, not the listener. This is accomplished by the use of "I statements." An "I statement" provides the listener information about what is going on inside the speaker's head, and what they may want from the listener.

A good speaker never starts their sentences with "you," because of the confrontation, implied accusation, and implied challenge this conveys. In couples' treatment, I tell my speakers to simply make a request of their partner such as, "I'd like to go out more on Saturday nights with you." If the speaker is unsure that the listener has heard them accurately, I might request that the listener mirror back the words to the speaker to let them know that they have been heard accurately. The mirroring process, while seeming a bit mechanical and simplistic, can be quite effective.

Do Not Raise Your Voice

Raising your voice to your partner kills dialogue and activates regressive tendencies. Babies and primitive humankind have in common tonal communication, which preceded verbal communication or language. Raised tones generally indicate distress situations, sometimes calling for fight or flight. We still have the same adrenal gland as the "cavemen" and it will react to a raised voice by pumping adrenaline throughout our system—we breathe faster, our heart races, and our bodies poise to fight or flee. This is hardly a state in which to practice effective conflict resolution. When voices rise, communication stops and distress begins.

If You are in a Deficit State, Postpone Your Interactions

A deficit state is any biopsychosocial condition that renders you less than your optimum, particularly in your interactions with others. The familiar HALT acronym (hungry, angry, lonely, tired) is but a beginning paradigm and yellow flag when to recognize that you are not at your best. The truth is that the list of deficits is much longer. Conscious self-knowledge of any deviation from your steady state will help you to postpone important interactions in your relationship. Simply let your partner know what's "going on" with you, that you don't feel well and request a "rain check" to resume the interaction soon thereafter.

Avoid Cursing or Name-Calling in a Relationship

Cursing and name-calling are notorious firebombs in a relationship. These poison utterances always wound, always arouse the potential for profound resentment in the other, and always run the risk of making flare-ups into full-blown arguments.

Frustration can produce some tense moments best met with silence. Ongoing cursing will be sure to irritate your partner, even disgust them. Cursing often makes you less attractive as a partner. Of particular offense are cursing adjectives insensitively used, like your "damn aunt."

How you would feel if someone referred to your relatives this way?

Name-calling is hurtful, intentional damaging communication and should be met with zero-tolerance in yourself and from others. Name-calling harkens back to a time in your childhood when your communication skills were so limited that the politics of shame and pain were handled through ridicule and disparaging names. Name-calling always diminishes both parties. Name-calling is never civil, never clever, and never in humor.

Steve and Pearl were on their way to catch a plane for the Caribbean. Steve, having forgotten it was rush hour, took the main thoroughfare, and wound up in a traffic jam. Pearl said, "boy, was that a stupid choice." Can you imagine how that comment made Steve feel? You can be sure Steve heard that not only was his choice stupid, he was stupid!

Socialite partners Gilbert and Ron were having dinner at a posh restaurant. As the wine steward approached with the wine list, Ron winked, chuckled, and said, "give it to me, he's an imbecile with wines." How did Gilbert feel?

The newest version of name-calling in this psychologically "sophisticated" age we live in is name-calling by psychiatric diagnosis. Not only is the recipient demeaned by the name, they are also diagnosed with a mental illness. Common quips that drip with diagnostic poison are things like "you're so anal," "you are so codependent," you drink just like your father," "you have an anger management problem," "you're abusive," and so on. Name-calling by diagnosis accomplishes double damage to your partner and your relationship.

Busy Couples Must Schedule Regular Meeting Times

This means uninterrupted times devoted solely to speaking and listening (on a frequent, regular basis) about all the "business" that the relationship needs to consider. This may consist of finishing up old business, determining the cooperative efforts versus division of labor, taking on current business, and beginning to discuss new business. Regular meetings force couples to deal with issues efficiently and non-neglectfully. One particular couple in treatment was helped to get out of enormous credit card debt by committing to regular weekly meetings.

Recreational Drugs Cloud and Often Darken a Relationship

The basis for recreational drug use is that everyday sober consciousness is not enough. People do drugs to cover their emotional pain as well. In essence, if someone is really okay, there is no need or basis for drug use. A shared cup of coffee or glass of wine are not considered "drugs." Drugs are any chemicals—legal or illegal—that significantly alter consciousness or cause intoxication. Drugs cause confusion, distortion, pain, and unreality to relationship maintenance. Drug use adds a problem to a problem.

Exercise Self-Control.

The vast majority of damage in relationships would be eliminated if more self-control were exercised. Problems with self-control differ from reactivity in that the former has more to do purely with your impulse control outside of and regardless of your partner's behavior.

I have a patient whose husband exercises very little self-control in his relationship to food and business ventures. He is obese and the couple is money-challenged quite often. In this case, he is quite loving and nonreactive with his wife, but his lack of self-control causes him and his relationship to have problems.

Be Aware of Your Relationship's "Black Holes"

Like individuals with assets and liabilities, relationships have their good and bad points. Couples are like snow flakes—they each have their own unique configuration. In this tool, both partners should stay acutely aware of their relationship's "character defects." (Character defects are the "unique" dysfunctional interactive behaviors endemic to that relationship.) These character defects are like black holes. They suck all the available energy around them while creating damaging implosion. One couple might bicker (quibble). Another couple might litigate (debate who's right). Yet another couple might lapse into states of mutually pained distance. Both partners have the collaborative responsibility to the relationship to know when they are headed for a "black hole," and change course so they will not fall into it.

Watch Your Nonverbal Behavior

Remember that your earliest communication was nonverbal. The facial expressions of others—especially their eyes—were some of the first ways you could tell, as a baby, that things were okay or not. Then came tones, gestures, and, eventually, words and language. Nonverbal behavior still lies deep in the roots of our communications.

We need to monitor our body language for gestures, expressions, mannerisms, and particularly our eye management as responsible partners. Eye contact is important and powerful as a communication tool. Good eye contact enhances listening and shows attention and respect to the speaker: be sure to use it.

We all have libido and regardless of our relationship status, we might feel sexual attraction towards a third party. Feelings that spontaneously arise cannot be helped. How you manage your feelings and nonverbal behavior is another matter. Our eyes are our windows to the outside world and what we see in that world. In counseling couples, I have spent a great deal of time helping them to distinguish between a glance and a stare. A glance is gazing at another person as one of many stimuli that occupy our current visual field. A stare is when we fix our gaze at another person long and focused enough to give that third party rather obvious importance. Staring at a third party is disrespectful to your partner and invites jealousy, resentment, and anxiety in them. In my experience, women have better eye management skills than men, although this is culturally driven. Men need to improve this skill, over which they are entirely responsible.

Vigilance is our First Task of Daily Relationship Maintenance

The proper piloting of a ship demands ongoing observation of where our vessel is going. We want it to get to the proper destination and we want it to get there safely. Would we ask any less of our relationship? Watch where you're going.

Quicken the Recovery Time after Conflict

Since people are not perfect, neither are relationships. There will be times when there will be interludes of tension, flare-up, and argument. How long that interlude lasts and how quickly it dissipates is entirely up to both of you! Four of the major enemies of good recovery time are:

- Self-righteous indignation
- Haughty pride
- Grudge-holding
- Vengefulness

Self-Righteous Indignation. "Look how I was treated when I did the right thing." Although you may be right, harboring this feeling will eventually eat you alive. The antidote to this indignation is to realize and accept that the world or life itself is not concerned with or about being "fair." Self righteous indignation is only sanitized resentment.

Haughty Pride. "The heck if I'm going to lower myself to apologize. Boy, will I look weak if I admit I'm wrong…the hell with them." Look back over your life and ponder how well your pride has served you.

Grudge Holding. "I'm never going to forget what he/she did to me. They're my enemy forever." Has this been helpful to your relations?

Vengefulness. "I'm going to get them back exactly like they got me. Let them feel exactly the way I feel." Has this feeling helped you to move on and live in the present moment? Hardly!

For any couple seeking to quicken the recovery time after an acute conflict, mastery over these four obstacles is absolutely essential. Self-righteous indignation, pride, grudge holding, and vengefulness fuel hostile, silent withdrawal—commonly known as the "cold-shoulder." This is one of the cases where silence is NOT golden: it is a vicious weapon. Deliberately distancing your partner to keep them "out in the cold" or in the "dog house" is abuse and emotional abandonment. It is harmful like any other kind of abuse and will damage the relationship.

Stop Repeating: Mastering the Repetition Compulsion in Relationships

One of Sigmund Freud's greatest contributions to the understanding of human behavior was his concept of the "the repetition compulsion." Although the concept existed before his time, Freud used psychoanalytic thought to further clarify why people unconsciously repeat patterns of behavior originating in their childhood, time and time again, throughout their life cycle.

In relationship maintenance, we must understand that the "repetition compulsion" is a problem that may certainly affect partners. The term "baggage" applies to maladaptive patterns of "old" behavior left over from a recently ended relationship. However, the "repetition compulsion" is a concept far broader and deeper than "baggage" because it brings its explanations of our repeating back to our earlier childhood origins.

The core idea of the "repetition compulsion" is that we can interact with others in one or both of the following ways: (1) we continue what happened to us as children, or (2) we try to get as adults, what we did not get as children.

Cybernetics comes to our aid today in further refining this concept. In many ways, the human mind is like a computer: it downloads experience. The earliest programs "installed" become the foundation programs established. These programs are utilized by us as children as soon as we can apply them to our need to function and develop. We tend to unconsciously and automatically use our early downloads again and again in interaction, not really asking ourselves about the utility of this old software. All we consciously know is that we want to get something and/or we're afraid we'll lose it; this is the simplest way to put it for your benefit in this book. Unless we become conscious ("get it") of programming and add new software to change, of course we will repeat. What else is there to draw on?

You can appreciate the problem this can create in managing an effective relationship. True reality testing between people can only occur by accurately receiving and understanding information occurring in the here and now. If you are still under the influence of repeating what happened or what you wish had happened as a child, how can you possibly understand your partner with any clarity, reality, or effectiveness? You need to be sufficiently "clear" and "emptied out" of past influence to be in the here and now.

Mastering the repetition compulsion involves remembering what happened. It means becoming conscious of what occurred, and the decision about living you made because of what occurred. It has nothing to do with blaming your parents. It has to do with what happened. When you remember and feel the feelings that shaped your early self you become aware. The repetition compulsion is unfinished business: when you become conscious and aware of this business, you can stop repeating it.

Mastering the repetition compulsion also means knowing that you are drawn to what you are familiar with, not simply in general, but in relationships in specific. Even if your early influences were abusive, traumatic, and damaging, that's what you "got" (what you experienced), and that's what you're familiar with. Do not underestimate the powerful allure of familiarity: it is the tendency of the human mind to organize new incoming data into known categories and function along those lines. This is the reason you project (or think you see) certain qualities onto that new person in your life. Additional information about the new person may change your idea about them. This may disappoint you that the new person is not who you thought they were. That is not their fault—it's simply that they were products of an idea that you "made" them with.

Home Cooking

People can split off and repress or deny the pain of their childhood and recall only fond recollections. A person might remember the smell of apple pie once baked by a mother who was usually too drunk to even get off the sofa. The child, now grown, may pay special attention to this smell, out of thousands of other competing stimuli. No matter who the current "chef" or "baker" of the pie is, this grown child will be drawn by the smell of the "home cooking," because of the comforting familiarity that it represents.

Some grown children in relationships smell apple pie when there's no smell at all. Some grown children smell apple pie when the real smell is sulfur and brimstone. Some grown children spend their lives—their entire lives—trying to track down that old sweet smell of apple pie.

Living in the here and now produces relationship health because it is founded on better reality testing. Mastering (and being mindful of) the allure of "home cooking" is of extreme importance in achieving relationship health.

9

Relationships and Self Esteem

The person we bring into our lives is a reflection of what we feel we deserve.

A woman recently came in to see me to figure out "what to do" with her marriage. She had one previous separation in their six-year-old relationship, which was for the same reasons that she sought help presently. Her husband had beaten her. He would often go out with his male friends and stay out all night. When he spent the night at home, he was drunk more often than not.

When she broke up with him two years ago, he begged her to return. He promised he would be a new man. She accepted his pleas and promises. She never asked him how he planned to change. She accepted his idea, and went on with life thinking he would become the man he promised he would be. Two more years of the same unchanged behavior on his part forced her to feel enough discomfort and pain to question the idea that he had changed. She was beaten again. She was left alone to do the household chores. Again, he was drunk almost every evening, and spent many evenings out on the town all night.

So here she was now, in therapy trying to decide whether she should stay with him or not. She told me he had said that he would really change this time—he really meant it. She didn't need to see one of those crazy, greedy therapists. He had finally seen the light.

The meager self-esteem of this woman suggests that she would ask for and be satisfied with so little. Her parents were alive and still had a happy and long-lived marriage. One would expect that she would activate what she "downloaded" and acquire, achieve, and maintain a happy, egalitarian, and nonabusive relationship. The "catch" was that as a little child, she was a pudgy girl of average intelligence who really wasn't accepted by her parents. Her mom and dad were attractive, fit, bright, and highly accomplished. They loved each other very much and spent a great deal of time together. They would try to be patient with their daughter, but really couldn't relate to her. The truth was that they were more comfortable when she was away from them playing with the few friends she had. She really knew this and it affected her self-esteem. Her idea of love became involvement with someone who left her out.

The psychological foundation of self-esteem you bring to relationships is predicated on these basic factors:

- Early parental, marital, or caregiver relationships you witnessed as a child, and internalized. These are the relationship imagos downloaded into your head.

- Your experience and meanings that you concluded about yourself and your worth. This is based on what you thought the significant others of your childhood felt about you. It is also based on your experience not just about what you concluded had happened, but what really happened.

- Any inner factors that you were born with such as illnesses, aptitudes, attributes, and constitution that would affect the evolution of your self-esteem. An autistic child born to average parents will indelibly have their childhood colored because of their condition. (We are not considering the parental reaction now; we are considering the condition of the child.) Any highly unusual inborn state for the child (genius, giantism, precocious development) additionally affects the unfolding of their childhood.

10

Special Relationship Conditions and Choices

The Love-Addicted Relationship

Although the impact of addiction on a relationship will be dealt with elsewhere, the love-addicted relationship deserves special attention in its own right.

Love-addicted people cannot tolerate being without a relationship. Many describe these people as dependent, but the dynamic in the relationship goes beyond dependency: love-addiction rules out well-being on one's own, or living life as a "single person."

The love-addicted couple (or person) really is suffering from an attachment disorder. Any separation from the other is met with enormous anxiety, a state of "non-well-being" and many of the signs that are seen with drug withdrawal. Such signs include severe longing to reattach in order to feel better, personal malaise, anxiety, sweating, abdominal distress, cardiac palpitation, and depression.

Love-addicted couples have an obsessive relationship with each other. Separation or potential separation carries such an enormous prospect of pain that jealousy and fear are constant companions. Although it might be tempting to describe love-addicted people as insecure, this fails to grasp a full understanding. Love-addicted people appear to have a developmental arrest that can't conceive of people being separate and feeling okay and intact. They seek fusion and constant togetherness because that is what most resembles a satisfactory state. They see their partner as necessary and mandatory versus some-one volitional, optional, and discretionary.

Love addicts, therefore, can live in some extremely abusive conditions because they feel they must be in a relationship. Because aloneness is to be avoided at all costs, love addicts manifest themselves as clingy, needy, insecure, jealous, and controlling. When both partners are love-addicted, their pathology is often masked (because they both want the same thing) and appears as "24/7" partners in a state of unending togetherness.

Anyone who feels a need for "space" and alone time will find the obsessiveness of a love addict engulfing and suffocating. They may even feel trapped and stalked: two well-known films that portray love addiction are "Play Misty for Me" and "Fatal Attraction."

Love addicts may deny their problem and comport their lives with their "other half" as if to say, "love conquers all."

The truth in these relationships is that "love is the drug." Relationship—or love-addiction, in fact, is an obsessive living hell that causes endless suffering. Love addiction requires treatment.

The On-Again, Off-Again Couple (or the OA-OA Couple)

OA-OA couples are characterized by a torturous roller coaster pattern highlighted by the relative inability to remain close over time. The features of this pattern reveal a cycle consistent enough to describe:

- A varying period of relative calm.

- The occurrence of a "difference" between the individuals, which escalates to an argument and/or withdrawal.

- Further escalation into an actual breakup.

- An ensuing period with each individual feeling various measures of emotional pain, self-justification, and feelings of being misunderstood.

- As time goes on, feelings of loss and longing for each other begin to dominate the time spent apart.

- The longing, which is often mutual, becomes profound and painful enough for one or both of the individuals to initiate contact with the other.

- A shaky reconnection is begun. It is infused with relief of loneliness, feelings of contrition, redeclaring of love, and concurrent fears of another blowup or breakup.

The OA-OA couple lives its life trapped in a cycle that rekindles itself with loneliness and chemistry and dismantles itself with conflict, resentment, and distance. These characteristics eventually take on a life of their own, and the dark forces of the OA-OA dynamics overshadow each partner's shaky autonomy.

I have treated OA-OA couples who have been "at it" for many, many years. The OA-OA cycle ultimately becomes "normal" for them—in effect, a life style. The participants feign mastery over the relationship, claiming they can predict what happens next, but their prediction is really familiarity with something they have little healthy control over.

In striking contrast to healthy relationships, the OA-OA couple does not grow, develop, change, and evolve in a linear fashion. The OA-OA couple goes in circles—all of its movement goes back to the point of origin, not someplace new.

OA-OA couples usually know that there's something "wrong." Sometimes they hear it from their friends or family. The psychological roots of this cycle are as varied as snowflakes. The participants may sense the "wrongness" and pathology, but often state—quite accurately—they have little if any power to "pull out."

There is no predictable or usual endpoint in the OA-OA cycle. Generally, the best thing that can happen is that the couple gets competent professional attention for themselves.

The Addicted Relationship

The Addict and Co-Dependent. Addiction is a disorder that is marked by the mishandling of discomfort. Addiction can be as mild as a compulsive moment. It can be as severe as an uncontrollable disease. Worse yet, addiction can begin to run rampant and attain a life and momentum of its own: even when the addict feels no discomfort, the addiction may growl for attention and expression through the person's behavior.

The outward manifestations of addiction may appear differently: ingestive addictions like drugs, alcohol, smoking, food, etc, or expressive addictions like gambling, compulsive sex, shopaholism, and workaholism. Professionals have realized that the outer and inner manifestations of the addiction must be addressed and confronted for abstinence and recovery to occur. True sobriety and transformation cannot proceed until the addict realizes that he or she is the core problem.

Addicts need (or feel they need) to mask the pain and unpleasure that most people are able to consciously feel, bear, and process.

Professionals, workers, and laypersons in the field of treating addictions soon realized some crucial facts about addiction in a relationship:

- Whatever the external manifestation of the illness, active addicts are "crazy" and lead a crazy destructive life.

- Anyone who enters into relationship with an active addict takes on this crazy life.

- Anyone who chooses this kind of life and puts up with it must have something terribly wrong with him or her as well. This is the reason why self-help organizations such as Al-Anon and CODA came into existence. They offer the help necessary for these people to get well, and stay well.

Crisis, suffering, and pain occur constantly in the addicted relationship. Addiction is incurable. If it is active, it inevitably is progressive and is either fatal, life threatening, or life destroying. Life for an addict is very difficult. They cannot accept "life on life's terms." They lie. They care only for themselves and have an inability to understand any kind of partnership. They are restless, irritable, and discontented. One of the major symptoms of addiction is disordered relations with their "fellow men." Therefore, it automatically follows that a relationship with any active addict is a sick, torturous experience.

The "Crazy Love" Relationship

Two essential ingredients for successful relationships are a "gratifying mix" and compatibility of values and behaviors. One element of a "gratifying mix" is a sense of chemistry. Chemistry refers to a strong sexual or erotic attraction.

A "crazy love" relationship is one that is almost totally dominated by a potent, overpowering and sometimes progressive sexual attraction between two specific people. This is to be contrasted with the sexually addicted relationship, where the participants are inherently unable to control their sexual impulses, regardless of the partner. Nymphomania, exhibitionism, and cruising are examples of sexual addiction. Although a "crazy love" relationship can be considered sexually-addicted, it is specific to that relationship only, and stems from the multiple levels of contact, fantasy, and arousal with a specific partner.

These relationships have no sense of conscious choice, logic, or compatibility of value. They follow an extremely dramatic, intense, colorful, and uneven course. Their sole nutrition relies on a fiery fuel and the prospect of ignition, combustion, explosion, and burnout is extremely high.

Two films that embody relationships that have elements of "crazy love" are "9 ½ Weeks" and "The Bridges of Madison County." The relationships in these works are hinged on chemistry, not compatibility. The elements of a crazy love relationship often carry the prospect of a short "shelf life." As information begins to emerge through the gaps of passion, the viability of these relationships are inevitably called into question and severely challenged.

The Arrangement

In contrast to crazy love, the arrangement is a relationship that is predicated on, and dominated by, practical, pragmatic, and logical concerns. It is a relationship that is "reality-intensive": the opposite of crazy love.

Arrangement relationships have little or no "chemistry," nor do they have a necessarily "gratifying mix" as their foundation. The core of arrangements lies rather on the tangible, measurable "gains" of being together as opposed to being apart. This is not to say that the gains are meager, unimportant, or lack meaning. To the contrary, factors such as comfort, routine, security, children, companionship, finances, and social opinion are indeed important and have every reason to be given careful consideration.

Often, romantics assume quite incorrectly that after the "honeymoon" (the courtship period), relationships usually degrade into arrangements. Nothing could be less true. Hopefully, couples will have made good estimates of compatibility and gratifying interrelatedness long before any fantasy-based intoxication will have worn off. Compatible couples make each other feel good because of who they are together and how they choose to behave. These "good feelings" are the basis of the relationship. Practical concerns that surround the arrangement relationship are of secondary importance to the compatible relationship.

Arrangement relationships are most stable when the practical considerations are conscious. If two people choose a relationship because together they are less lonely and they can also boost their purchasing power, let them openly discuss it. When the basis of this or any other relationship is conscious choice, it is inherently more manageable. Arrangement relationships need not require loving feelings as a basis, but do need fondness and a conscious intent. To care for each other is necessary, so the arrangement does not degrade into a hollow bargain.

Relationships with Physically or Mentally Ill Partners

Illness—physical or mental—can "visit" the relationship in the following ways.

- One can knowingly choose an ill partner for a relationship.
- One or both partners can grow ill during the life of the relationship.
- A combination of these situations can occur.

For your purposes, illness is defined as a pathological condition that is neither transient nor mild. A stroke would be an illness; a common cold would not. The illnesses that affect relationships are sicknesses, conditions, and maladies that visit and stay.

Knowingly Choosing An Ill Partner. This is a major decision that must be made only after the most thorough research. This means your getting the most accurate information possible about the actual illness or condition of the potential partner. (The specifics of this inquiry are dealt with in great detail later in this chapter in the section "choosing a partner.") Of equal importance is the reaction of the potential partner to their condition or illness: have they "accepted" their illness or are they still in turmoil about it? Do they utilize optimal professional and/ or self-care, so the illness is not worsened?

When Someone in the Relationship Grows Ill. This is one of the greatest losses and challenges a relationship can cope with. There is a strong ethical norm in our society that supports caregiving of the sick partner by the well partner. Sometimes the emotional impact of adjustment and actual care provision by the well partner can be enormous beyond words. Consider the profound rigors of taking care of a dwindling partner afflicted with Alzheimer's disease, terminal cancer, or AIDS. Though these very same caregivers would generally not choose to enter a relationship with people this ill, the mandates of personal caring, love, and commitment keep them involved when illness strikes their relationship.

It is extremely important that optimal care, nurturing, and structure be available and utilized by both the ill and the well partner. The caregiver's support, rest, and free time are of equal necessity to the medical care of the ill partner.

Choosing a Partner

In order to make this choice, you need complete information about the other person. The following categories are essential data:

- Your partner's personal history;

- Your partner's family history;

- Any exposure to trauma your partner may have had (i.e., abuse, accidents, alcoholism in a parent);

- Any personal history (featuring) a chronic physical or mental illness your intended partner had or has; and

- How all of the above may have affected their prior relationships.

This reiterates one of the pillars of wise relationship choices—you need lots of accurate information so that you can make good choices and avoid needless suffering.

Your Partner's Personal History. Everything that comprises your partner's prior life can be generally reduced to two factors. One is their genetic endowment—what they're born with. Examples of this are intelligence and body type. The other factor is everything they've experienced. This means all the environmental stimuli they've been exposed to before meeting you. Indeed, it's important for you to be mindful of what's "happened" to your potential partner. Many of my oldest patients "went through" the Great Depression, and all of these unfortunates were affected mentally in some way: anxiety over having "enough" and a neurotic frugality were predominant symptoms, although many of these people never truly experienced poverty.

Your Partner's Family History. This important information focuses on the gene pool they came from. One's genetic heritage is relevant here as possible predisposition to illness (i.e., biologically based mood disorders) and outright risk of illness (i.e., Huntington's Chorea, Tay-Sachs disease). It's important to know if your intended partner is at risk of hereditary-based illness.

Any Exposure to Trauma Your Partner May Have Had. Trauma is any experience that leaves emotional and psychological scar tissue on an individual. Trauma can cause psychiatric disorders such as post-traumatic stress disorder, acute stress disorder, paranoid states, "hoarding," phobias, chronic insecurity, and aggressivity (abuse-giving) disorders. Trauma is outside the realm and experiences of everyday life.

Examples of loss-based trauma are Hurricane Andrew, sudden infant (crib) death syndrome, and fatal accidents. Examples of intent-based trauma are rape, incest, and verbal and physical abuse. Mass traumas such as 9/11 carry both intent and loss as elements of their origin and impact.

People that have been traumatized are people that have been deeply and perhaps permanently scarred by extraordinarily negative events. Relationship choices must absolutely take this into consideration.

Traumas can have a negative "rippling" effect down through the generations. I have treated perhaps a dozen children of Holocaust survivors. It was evident that the Holocaust had scarred these survivors so badly that as parents, they emotionally damaged their own offspring.

Any Personal History of Chronic Physical or Mental Illness Your Partner Has or Had. I have counseled patients who have had chronic physical illnesses such as diabetes, rheumatoid arthritis, cancer, heart disease, hypertension, stroke, fibromyalgia, lupus, scleroderma, and multiple sclerosis. Chronic physical diseases can be categorized as to whether they are:

- Treatable (diabetes) vs. untreatable (Huntington's Chorea);

- Progressive (Alzheimer's disease) vs. nonprogressive (stroke);

- Fatal (Alzheimer's disease, terminal cancer) vs. non-fatal (arthritis);

- Incurable (multiple sclerosis) vs. "curable" (hypertension, melanoma)

- Incurable but manageable (AIDS, diabetes);

- Incurable and hard to manage (Alzheimer's disease).

Chronic physical illness can have such a profound effect on the life of a relationship that the condition itself seems like a living entity and third party.

Mental disorders and illnesses can wreak havoc on a relationship as well. Mild mental disorders such as "adjustment disorders" are expected to have far less impact on a couple because of their time-limited nature. The vast majority of mental illnesses are treatable, with the exception of the "neurologically based" illnesses such as Alzheimer's disease and Huntington's Chorea. Mental illnesses should be categorized as to whether they are:

- Progressive (Alzheimer's disease) vs. nonprogressive (generalized anxiety disorders);

- Fatal (Alzheimer's disease) vs. nonfatal (depressive mood disorders);

- Incurable (schizophrenia) vs. curable (phobias);

- Incurable but manageable (Bipolar disorders);

- Incurable and hard to manage (Alzheimer's disease, Schizophrenia).

In this age of pop psychology, it seems that people feel qualified to diagnose their partner's mental state to them, although they would rarely attempt to do the same for physical problems. However, everyone should have a simple working knowledge of mental illness for recognition sake. The easiest way for you to understand mental illnesses as it affects relationships is to group them into two types:

- The ego dystonic illnesses cause great suffering and symptoms with a corresponding wish to feel better, get better, and change.

- The ego syntonic illnesses affect the personality and cause difficulties with other people. The ill person may have no obvious self-distress. Indeed, the person may not feel ill at all, and may attribute any interpersonal problems to others around them. Consequently, there is no strong wish to feel better, get better, or change.

The following data will be of help to you by providing more detailed information about each group of mental disorders.

The ego dystonic (suffering) illnesses can be grouped into the milder neuroses and the more severe psychoses. Both groups of these illnesses are disturbing and/or painful. The sufferer wants help to be rid of them. From this point of view, the ego dystonic illnesses carry a better prognosis from a relationship point of view, as a treated illness should have less negative impact on the couple.

Common examples of everyday neuroses are phobias, generalized anxiety disorders, obsessive-compulsive disorders, and depressive neuroses (or dysthymias). These illnesses can be successfully treated with psychotherapy and/or medication.

Psychoses are much more severe in that they are characterized by impaired reality testing. When they are accompanied by delusions and hallucinations, the person may be so sick that they are lost in an inner world and may not be capable of realistic interactions with their partner.

Examples of psychotic illnesses are the schizophrenic illnesses and the manic phase of manic-depressive disorder (Bipolar I disorder). Some psychotic patients are so sick that they don't even know how to take care of themselves. These extremely disruptive symptoms quickly compel the patient's, partner's, or family's attention in getting prompt professional attention.

The initial treatment of a psychotic patient is to stabilize them and get them functioning: generally this involves hospitalization and medication. Psychotic disorders are considered chronic, relapsible, and serious—patients may need medication and psychotherapy on a relatively permanent basis to maintain stability. The impact of psychosis on a relationship can be extremely severe.

It is often clear, however, to most neurotic and psychotic people that something is wrong with them, and a problem acknowledged is a problem that can be helped.

The *ego-syntonic* ("non-suffering") illnesses are the personality disorders. As stated earlier, these disorders carry the worst prognosis. Although these patients are non-psychotic, they are at odds with the world around them most of the time. Examples of the personality disorders are the narcissistic personality, borderline personality, passive dependent personality, and the histrionic personality. Rather than feel genuine personal pain, these unfortunates act out their dysfunction. They may sense there is a problem, but usually blame it on sources outside of themselves. Therefore, meaningful therapy is usually out of the question for these people.

Do you see any physical or mental illness in a potential partner? If so, list the symptoms below:

11

Requesting and Compromising

These two activities will form the core of how you can effectively navigate and negotiate the often-varied needs of you and your partner.

Requesting

Requesting is done in very specific ways. It is a two-step process that you may need to learn. It consists of informing your partner of what you are feeling and what you want. In contrast to the war-like demand ("you will go to the…"), requesting will begin as an "I" statement.

A request is your ticket to an intentionally tactful interactive moment. You might say, "I'm starting to get hungry (the feeling)." "I'd like to go out to eat with you as soon as you feel like it (what you want)."

Some people misunderstand that a request is a simple question put to your partner. To repeat, a request is far more effective when you first inform you partner what you are feeling, as this lays a tangible foundation for what you want from them.

Compromising

It is inevitable that partners often have different sets of needs at any given moment. There must be a method of navigating those contrasting needs. The most effective and time-tested tool of needs negotiation is compromise. This process is a good-will driven effort that ensures that both partners will be satisfied in some measure. It involves each partner as a polarity modifying their needs in the direction of their partner. Compromising is a win-win process. To follow-up on the above example, if the second partner is not hungry and doesn't expect to be, they might say, "I'm not expecting to be hungry, but let's go out and I'll have something light." This is compromise.

12

Your "Tackle Box" and Your Relationships

All of us carry around a tackle box, but yours is thoroughly unique and specific to you. You are born with one set of tackle box components: these are the assets and liabilities that are hereditary and genetically determined. Examples of genetic assets might be high intelligence or rapid motor skills. Examples of genetic liabilities might be nearsightedness or a tendency towards obesity.

Your second set of tackle-box components are the things that you've experienced, both "good" and "bad." It is generally agreed this begins at birth with your first "waking" moments. Consider your brain to be something like a computer that is downloading as you leave your mother's protective womb and you enter the external world of "reality." These good" and "bad" tackle-box components of course will be changing and increasing with each new experience. Therefore, at any given moment, your tackle-box contents are comprised of:

- Your genetic endowment;

- All that's happened to you "until this very moment";

- How you reacted to what has happened, which includes your conclusions and beliefs about yourself and your life.

For instance, your tackle box around the mid-teen years is considered to be in a state of "prerelationshiphood"—this means the entirety of your being (or contents) that you will bring to your first "adult" relationship.

You will bring your tackle box with you everywhere you go, and this includes every one of your relationships.

Like the fisherman's tackle box, its important for you to know what you've got inside because you cannot pull something out of your tackle box that is not there. A successful fisherman has a tackle box which has a complete set of organized tools, tackle, and items that they must keep and utilize to achieve good results.

Like that of a successful fisherman, your ideal tackle box should:

- Have all the necessary tools and tackle you'll need to be prepared for the specific "work";

- Have sufficient variation of tools for different kinds of work;

- Be used flexibly and intelligently;

- Be adaptable—one tool may be great in one case, but terrible in another case;

- Must be kept free of rust, water, dirt, and salt, and in good working order (any rusty item must be refurbished or replaced, lest it "infect" other items;

- Be stocked with items and tools that are needed in an emergency.

Remember, however, that your tackle box is inside you. Unlike the angler's tackle box, you cannot go out and quickly buy tools and items at the tackle shop. These tools are not for sale. Be especially cautious of "tackle shops" offering marvelous tools easily obtainable over a weekend, but at very high prices.

For each "angling effort," plan on knowing if your tackle box really has the necessary tools to meet the tasks and achieve success. This will not only save the (finite) amount of lifetime you have. It will also save you heartache and suffering.

I recall one patient quite clearly. He was a physician who was at the peak of professional practice. Money was no longer a problem. He had put his personal life on hold because of his training and his medical duties. Now in his mid-forties, he was "ready for love."

He had recently met a twenty-five-year-old Swedish beauty queen at a social function. She was surrounded by handsome young men. He introduced himself to her and later told me it was "love at first sight." His subsequent inquiries revealed she had a penchant for fast-living, stunning men, yet his determination to have her was great. He pursued her relentlessly, and courted her. He used his impressive wealth to offer her delights and exotic experiences far beyond the reach of her younger courtiers.

She was initially bedazzled and responded fully to his promises of alluring distant shores. She even accepted his proposal of marriage in the midst of their heady, global adventures. Eventually, he had to return to his medical practice (this is who he was) and the marriage began to settle into an established routine. The trips tapered and the flair flattened into the light of cold day. She would see her new husband come home tired and gray: to her, he looked like an old man. She grew bored and took up with a jetset playboy closer to her own age. Soon, she moved out of the marital home.

This woman was looking for a tackle box full of fun, constant change, and excitement. My patient came to learn that his tackle box really never had the necessary tools to achieve success in this case. He learned through his suffering to be realistic about his tackle box: to fully know whether its contents were sufficient or whether he needed more tackle.

Another patient of mine had a long history of abuse and abandonment as a child. He recalled making a decision to "go it alone": it was safer that way. The years passed safely but were "empty," somehow: a large part of him yearned to have closeness with another. His early years of abuse and subsequent years of self-protective aloneness afforded him a shortage of the skills necessary to achieve real intimacy. His tackle box would have to be fuller than it was.

Adding to his tackle box involved dealing with the following unfolding realities:

- Realizing he could no longer live his life this way. This created a sense of necessity, urgency, and "surrender."

- His "surrender" meant that he knew he could not change his tackle box with what he had. He knew he would need help.

- The help that he would need should come from someone or something that could provide from their tackle box the qualities and tools that would help him change inside.

- He learned that this process took time and involved insight with tangible behavioral changes that were practiced often, honestly, and long enough to be effective. His early new behaviors felt like acting, but after a significant amount of time it felt real. Behavioral repetition in the face of initial discomfort slowly became new behaviors added into his tackle box.

The specific method of inner change that he chose was psychotherapy. The therapy focused on his resisting his impulse to run away to his illusion of safety whenever he felt scared, hurt, or disappointed by another person. It meant that he would have to bear his pain, stand still, and start to talk to other people about what he felt and what he needed. After being a certain way for so long, he knew these changes would take time to make—and they did! He learned in therapy to assess when he was really in danger, which was far less often than he initially thought. He learned in therapy to stop repeating old patterns of behavior that kept him stuck. He began to choose people that were truly more available and nurturing. He learned over a very long period to stop the mind clutter of self-defeating thoughts (rusty hooks from his tackle box), clear his head, and remain in the true here and now. In the face of discomfort, he forced himself to be with people, "stick" with them, and tolerate their inevitable imperfections.

This man really was able to add to his tackle box. His increased tools and skills did enable him to be up to the challenges of acquiring and maintaining a healthy, intimate relationship.

You can add to your tackle box, but only through solidly acquired and established changes that are internalized.

13

Relationship Skills

Relationship skills are the tools that build functional, deep relationships. The most important among them are:

- Self-ownership
- Good listening behavior
- Effective needs negotiation
- Ability to stay in the present moment
- Tolerance of differences
- On good behavior "forever"
- Golden silence
- Nonreactivity
- Ability to internalize and work through conflicts
- Readiness to provide emotional support
- Sensitivity to partner's feelings

Self-Ownership

If partners are willing to assume ownership of their own feelings and behaviors, a strong healthy foundation is created. If either partner feels bad, they are willing to embrace that feeling as theirs and will communicate that feeling to the other partner as theirs (i.e., "I'm worried about you driving in this storm").

In a healthy relationship, each partner not only assumes ownership of their feelings, they also assume responsibility when requesting their partner to help them manage their feelings. For example, "I'm worried about you driving in this storm. Can you call me when you reach your office?" This type of communication sets the tone for the "I" message which gives information about one's interior state to the partner.

Good Listening Behavior

Good listening creates an atmosphere of mutuality, respect, self-control, and communication simplicity. In relationships, good listening requires clearing one's mind and hearing the other person's utterances without any inner clutter.

Listening is an active process that can often be improved by mirroring back to the other person what was heard. For example, "I heard you say that you are worried about me driving in this storm, and I will try to call you as soon as I reach the office." This kind of mirroring validates that the communication was accurately received. Mirroring builds trust in relationships.

Effective Needs Negotiation

Each partner has their own special needs that, at times, inevitably differ from those of their partner. This occurs even in highly compatible relationships.

Effectiveness in gratifying these needs differences involves the old fashioned art of compromise. Compromise allows each partner's needs to be gratified in a smaller or postponed measure for the good of maintaining the relationship.

For example, a couple with different tastes in film may agree to see an action film one week and a philosophical art film the next week in order to gratify each partner in turn. Healthy needs negotiation involves the skill of transport between the polarities of self-assertiveness and flexibility. The core of this skill lies in each partner being sufficiently gratified personally to allow for compromise. This also means that each partner commits to being aware of the needs of the other and trying to gratify those needs. This takes work and energy: it may necessitate some temporary discomfort or self-sacrifice for the good of keeping the relationship in working order.

Ability to Stay in the Present Moment

One of the biggest sources of difficulty for couples is the inability to stay in the present moment. Distortions in the communication process are often caused by the listener contaminating the process with their inner historical issues. Problems they encountered in past relationships influence their behavior with their current partner.

It is essential to communication that both partners hear and understand exactly what the other is saying. The phenomenon of "transference" indicates that, at times, people inappropriately displace the past onto the present. Intimate relationships make the phenomenon of transference even more likely to occur.

Tolerance of Differences

No two people are alike. This is true in relationships with even the highest levels of compatibility. The most functional relationships strive to neutralize as many incompatibilities between the partners as possible, compromising the differences when possible, and tolerating the differences when not. Any difference between two people is a potential for conflict. Conflict breaks out when needs negotiations fail and tolerance is absent. The differences can seem to be trite: two partners may disagree over how cold an air conditioner should be running at night. Poor tolerance of differences can create distance between partners and may lead to isolation or even separate bedrooms. Good tolerance of differences will lead to temporary discomfort in a strengthened relationship.

On Good Behavior "Forever"

If you've ever had a flower garden, you know it must have sunlight, water, nutrients, and be combed clean of weeds and bugs. Deep relationships are gardens, too, and must be cared for in the same way.

Often people think relationships are self-maintaining and they stop giving the kind of tender loving care they gave when they were just getting started. But like a garden, lack of continued attention will cause a relationship to wither and die.

We should treat our deep relationships as if millions of people were watching us, twenty-four hours a day.

We should always be on good behavior in our relationships. The sunlight, water, and the nutrients of good behavior are tact, politeness, and gratitude.

Tact

Tact is constructed by thinking about our behavior—particularly our words—before we express it to our partner. That involves embracing the ownership and architecture of what we say and how we say it. Being tactful means planning and executing words and actions in a way that is sensitive to how our partner will feel as a result of our words or actions. Tact is a skill that can be learned at any point in the life cycle, despite our experience in our own family of origin.

Politeness

Politeness refers somewhat differently to the formal respect we show our partner. Politeness is shown when we use basic manners, such as saying "please" when we request and "thank you" when we receive. Politeness is a form of valuation we use to show our partner that we appreciate the efforts they make to please us.

Gratitude

Gratitude is far more than a polite thank you. It is an attitude that expresses our appreciation and satisfaction not just in a partner's efforts, but for who they are and for the radiance they bring to the relationship. Gratitude can be expressed in a million ways—in a word well chosen, in admiration of the color of their eyes, or through appreciation of their kindness to a child. The ways are endless.

Politeness is saying "thank you"; gratitude is being thankful.

Golden Silence

In deep relationships, words are often essential. At times, words can be counterproductive. There are many times when golden silence is appropriate in a relationship. Generally, if one partner knows that their words will only bring pain to the other, golden silence is best used until less harmful ways of communicating are found.

At times, golden silence contains potentially runaway conflicts by diffusing upward—spiraling escalation in highly reactive couples. Silence is also a wise response when one is unsure how to respond. Silence sets the stage for listening stance. It invites reflection.

Silence is a relationship tool whose use must be carefully thought through. Silence should not be used as a weapon of chilly rejection, anger, or withdrawal. Silence should not be used when a partner is asking for a verbal response unless one is buying time for that response.

One area that loving couples are often not silent enough about are past relationships. It is rarely necessary to share potentially harmful details of past relationships or make comparisons to one's current partner. This sets the stage for recrimination, resentment, pain, or retaliation. One element that can be useful to share is what one has learned of oneself from past relationships. This provides current information useful to a partner in understanding the dynamics of the current relationship without offering any painful details.

Nonreactivity

Nonreactivity is a special relationship skill that is dependent on one's temperament, communication style, frustration tolerance, listening ability, insight, and humility. It is one of the most challenging skills to develop and perfect in a relationship.

The leading cause of runaway conflict in a relationship is reactivity. Partners who are competitive, litigious, aggressive, and addicted to "being right" are at the highest risk for reactivity. This is a skill that needs constant monitoring in couples and relationships where flare-ups are an ongoing risk.

Nonreactivity is a behavioral skill that can be learned by practicing "golden silence" and deep breathing. This can be employed regardless of one's background, constitution, or beliefs. Rather than reacting aggressively to a conflict, nonreactive partners remain calm and quiet long enough to assess the situation. Nonreactivity immediately stabilizes the conflict into a transient state that can be processed rationally. Nonreactivity prevents destructive conflicts so that relationship order can prevail. Stormy relationships have little interest in curbing reactivity since this is one of the bases for relating to each other. Functional relationships, however, have no such interest in reactivity.

Ability to Internalize and Work Through Conflicts

When we are able to solve our problems internally, we sometimes feel some personal discomfort, but we avoid the potentially greater discomfort involving our partner in the conflict. For example, feeling an attraction toward other than our chosen partner creates conflict. Telling our partner about the attraction will inevitably cause discomfort or even distrust. If we are able to work through those feelings internally, we avoid escalating the conflict and straining the relationship. By internalizing the conflict, we achieve a greater simplicity in the relationship. Although partners can often offer support to one another during personal struggles, the relationship should not be the dumping ground for displaced frustration.

Sometimes partners are incapable of internalizing personal conflicts and they act out the conflict in the context of the relationship. For example, a man came home angry from his job and displaced his anger onto his wife. The job and its frustrations were the cause of his anger, but his relationship suffered because he could not internalize and work through his conflict. The relationship should not bear the emotional weight of his frustration.

A married woman was in therapy for a number of problems, including her wish to be with a more sensitive, passionate partner. Her husband made it clear he saw no problem with himself and had no need for change. Often the wife would flirt openly with other men or point out her husband's lack of "lust for life." This acting out in the marriage caused further complication and pain. Ideally, the wife needed to internalize the conflict and not flirt with other men. Internally, she needed to either accept her husband or leave the marriage.

Readiness to Provide Emotional Support

Firm relationships are maintained when it is clear to both parties that each is committed to providing the interventions necessary to help carry the other partner through a tough time. It also indicates that there is an active caring that increases comfort and safety for the relationship.

Sensitivity to Partner's Feelings

Sensitivity to the other partner's feelings is much like providing emotional support, but is more of a 24-hour-a-day effort. We are sensitive to our partner's feelings because they are important and because the attention we give underscores our daily demonstrable position to "tend the garden."

Which skills do you think you have mastered?

Which skills do you think you need to work on?

14

Barriers to Relationship Intimacy: "Avoid the Dirty Dozen"

1. Insufficient shared information creates a relationship vacuum and promotes guessing, projection, and suspicion.

Healthy relationship choices are the outcome of thorough relationship evaluations, which are based on the receipt of thorough, accurate information. You must fully know the data that you aim to process.

It is a psychological maxim that data and information "hook" a person's logic, provide structure, support healthier ego functioning, adaptation, and planning. Conversely, no data isolates you and throws you into an intrapersonal world full of hunches, suspicion, and inner mental meanderings.

The early experiments of people put in isolation or sensory deprivation chambers caused them to regress, hallucinate, and grow psychotic. These extreme examples indicate that true interpersonality and the facts attached to it support reality testing.

What you share with your partner is a germane consideration as well. Your best criterion for what is asked and what is answered is that information should be relevant and helpful, but never hurtful and damaging. As an experienced "relationship choice maker," you soon learn to know what is necessary and essential, and what is more than you or your partner need to know.

2. Incomplete prerelationship work creates a flood of unfinished business.

Nothing complicates a new relationship more than the unfinished business of an individual. As discussed elsewhere in this book, the three major elements that a person needs to "finish" (in a work-in-progress sense) are:

- A sense of completeness;
- Fulfillment of potential; and
- Ability to take care of oneself.

All of these features are your prerelationship work. This means that these three areas should be basically "taken care of" in large measure before entering a relationship.

The personal unhappiness that stems from relative incompletion of these three spheres will cause significant disturbance, and will slowly poison an unfolding relationship.

A healthy relationship is not composed of two halves, but rather two wholes.

3. Fear of Closeness Creates Distance and Isolation

The fear of closeness and intimacy has reached epidemic proportions in relationships. Why would someone be so afraid of becoming close to another person? The answer would reveal that the sufferer must believe that closeness and intimacy are dangerous and threatening to their well being. A possible origin of this fear might be that the person may have suffered a traumatic loss of a loved one or someone's love. Alternatively, the person may have witnessed their parents fighting and quarreling so often that they've concluded and believe that closeness is dangerous. While it is understandable that such a conclusion was reached, it is also premature and prejudicial: all relationships are not dangerous.

Fear of closeness is a phobia-driven illness, and its "cure" lies in progressive attempts to safely and methodically get closer to another person who is capable of doing the same. No relationship can survive in a healthy fashion when the fear of closeness exists in any measure.

Pursuing and attaining closeness with a loved one should proceed while facing the inevitable fact that you will ultimately lose them. It is the reality of impermanence that makes the pursuit and attainment of intimacy and closeness even more meaningful, worthwhile, and necessary.

4. Resentment and begrudgement invites wounding and sniping.

Resentment is an angry feeling towards another who you judge has significantly mistreated you. Resentment can grow from a preoccupation into an obsession that lasts for a lifetime. Resentment can also grow into begrudgement, which is a focus of ill will that objects to the good fortune of another. At worst, it's a wish for the suffering of someone who has hurt you.

When people in a relationship harbor resentment for each other, their "emotional field" becomes a hot zone with ongoing risks of flare-ups, arguments, and enmity. Minor problems become enlarged fights because the preexisting resentments and begrudgements find a foothold and ignite into a firestorm of controversy.

Just like cigarettes, resentment and begrudgement are poisons. They should be prevented or extinguished as soon as possible. The best ways of preventing these poisonous feelings is through the use of effective relationship skills. The best ways of extinguishing them is through effective conflict resolution.

5. Unwillingness to take behavioral ownership creates scapegoats and destroys a partnership.

In my recent work with a gay couple, one partner claimed to feel free to flirt with waiters in the cafes of South Beach, right in the presence of his "significant other." When that significant other spoke up and voiced his discomfort over the flirting, he was chided as being narrow-minded, possessive, and insecure. The flirting partner took no responsibility whatsoever for his behavior. Where is the basis for a healthy trusting partnership?

6. Too much historical baggage creates relationship cynicism and distorts the present moment.

One of the worst caricatures of this barrier is the multiply divorced person who is lost in a fog of chronic bitterness towards the opposite sex. They appear unable to "see" truly new experiences. All they can offer are generalizations that prove to be meager, clumsy, and incorrect in navigating the world of relationships. If they can "see" their baggage and "dump it," they can lead freer lives.

7. Mockery and devaluation of your partner kills love.

Couples want to be esteemed by each other. There is no excuse whatsoever for diminishing your partner. Mockery and devaluation are inevitably symptoms of anger, resentment, personal insecurity, fear, personal unhappiness, or pathological narcissism. If you feel the urge to put your partner down, refrain from it and try to find the source of this impulse. This will generally involve some unfinished personal or relationship business. Giving in to the impulse to mock and devalue your partner will eventually cause their love for you to wither away and die.

8. Addictive behavior creates damage, mistrust, and pain in a relationship.

This topic has been discussed elsewhere (special conditions in relationships), yet it will help to repeat some basic facts.

- No relationship can ever attain health in the presence of active addiction;

- Anyone who knowingly pairs up with an active addict is as sick and "crazy" as the addict;

- Addiction is incurable, but manageable when the addict is involved in some form of 12-step program. At a minimum, this requires going to meetings, getting a sponsor, "working" the Steps, and doing service. You should also be aware that psychotherapy alone as a treatment for addiction is woefully inadequate.

9. Hypersensitivity and emotional binging create a lack of control in the relationship.

Hypersensitivity can be defined as a "disorder" of feeling too quickly hurt, affected, and/or resentful in response to the events and discomforts of everyday life. Hypersensitive people are emotionally affected more easily and quickly than the vast majority of their peers. Hypersensitivity can arise from inherited constitution, depression, active drug and alcohol intoxication, and many other sources. Hypersensitive people have something "wrong" with them that they need to face, fix, and manage.

Emotional binging, in contrast, refers to manipulative behavior under conscious control, which overplays emotions regarding a given situation. Emotional binging reveals that the overdramatizing or exaggeration of feelings about a situation or event—such as an affront—is an attempt to "purchase" a secondary gain such as feeling like a wounded victim or martyr. People who emotionally binge need to control themselves and be more responsible, because the flooding and prolongation of excessive emotion in the couple eats away at the logic, intellect, and "science" that lays at the foundation of healthy relationships.

10. Poor needs negotiation creates conflict.

You recognize that all people are different, and that even the most compatible couple will have individual needs that differ at times. Effective management of differing needs takes a problem-solving approach that uses compromise and negotiation as its tools. Partners in a relationship who compromise often feel a sense of pride in sacrificing or modifying a need "downward" when they know it will satisfy and stabilize their partner and the relationship itself. Mutual giving flourishes in an atmosphere of cooperation.

When any of the above elements are absent by conscious choice or by lack of awareness, the satisfaction of individual needs in a relationship becomes more conflicted: a relationship loses its health when it becomes a battleground.

11. Reactivity creates runaway fighting and arguing.

A famous directive from Alcoholics Anonymous instructs you to "exercise restraint of tongue and pen." In contrast, reactivity is a mindless, thoughtless reflex and involves the least evolved, most primitive parts of yourself and your animal origins. Restraint is equated with thoughtful, conscious self-control and indicates better ego functioning. Soccer match riots epitomize the reactivity that leads to runaway fighting and even murder—a group becomes a mob. Restraint of reactivity minimizes the likelihood of rioting in a relationship.

12. Litigious behavior changes the relationship into a courtroom.

Litigious behavior stands alongside psychoanalyzing one's partner as the newest form(s) of "verbal violence" in a relationship. Specifically, litigious behavior is a deeply neurotic relationship dynamic in which one partner sets out to prove they are right and the other partner is wrong. The goal and method is inevitably one of competitive domination. Litigating in a relationship is different from mindless immature bickering. Litigating can hook a couple into an addictive competitive battle in which victory is sought through the intellectual and strategic conquest lawyers often use in court.

Litigating is to be avoided at all costs. Not only does it damage the goodwill in a relationship: it also creates the illusion that there is only one right way. Do you want to create a courtroom out of your relation-ship? Certainly not.

List any barriers to intimacy you have overcome.

List any barriers to intimacy you would like to overcome.

15

Measuring Your Relationship

This is the first of the three chapters that will provide you with a more graphic and schematic way of assessing your "deep relationships." The basis for assessing your relationships is to determine with clarity, honesty, and accuracy whether you are satisfied with your partner in relation to you.

There are two forms of self-inquiry you can engage in to measure your relationship satisfaction and involvement, both of which will also provide you with additional thinking about the relationships' health, functionality, and mutuality.

First, you should ask yourself often whether your partner's presence in your life is considered by you to be positive, neutral, or negative. I have called this device the "relationship handle." Not only does this give you a quick measure and inventory, it also points out potential problems and their need for improvement.

Second, you should also ask yourself whether you envision this person (your partner) in your life next year, in five years, in ten years, etc. This method cuts through denial, clarifies uncertainties, and offers a crude prognosis.

Measuring a relationship by self-inquiry is one of the simpler ways to determine relationship satisfaction. The following two chapters present more intricate relationship measures.

List important relationships in your life.

Do these people have a positive, neutral, or negative influence on your life?

Do you think you will still be involved in this relationship in 1 year? In 5 years? In 10 years?

16

A Compatibility Index for Couples

I've listed ten sets of polarities that describe frequently occurring personality features and attitudes in relationships. Because each polarity represents an extreme, you'll probably find that you and your partner could be somewhere "in the middle."

The value of this approach is that it pinpoints areas of contrast versus compatibility with relative clarity, as well as providing some basis of measurement. You will notice that the polarity sets have definite interrelationships and overlap.

Compatibility has been found to be perhaps the major factor in relationship longevity and satisfaction. If you and your partner found yourselves opposites in all ten categories, it would be reasonable to expect a high level of dissatisfying opposition between yourselves.

1. Logical versus Emotional

A logical person conveys and embraces a scientific approach that emphasizes tangibility and reason. Logical people can bring level-headed negotiation to relationships. An emotional person conveys and embraces an intuitive approach that emphasizes "gut" feelings. Emotional people can bring immediacy and inspiration to relationships.

2. The Self-Generator versus the Other-Directed

Self-generating people are essentially looking within themselves for insights, truths, and especially for operating priorities as to running their lives. Self-generating people are not necessarily selfish—they simply take what arises from within as primary. Therefore, a self-directed person in relationships emphasizes the effectiveness and necessity of what they want to communicate. Self-generators focus on the message.

In contrast, the other-directed person focuses more on how the message is received. More specifically, they draw on norms and socially derived values outside of themselves in shaping their attitudes and behavior. What other people think is a significant priority for the other-directed person, which causes them to send out strong social probes. These people emphasize tact in relationships.

3. Conflict Frontalist versus Conflict Avoider

A conflict frontalist is someone who actively pursues and "works" a conflict in order to resolve it. Such a person emphasizes active engagement of themselves and their partners to work through feelings and problems associated with the conflict. In a relationship dispute, fight, or argument, such a person can be expected to pursue the issue and their partner for conflict resolution. Any attendant discomfort is of lesser significance to the conflict frontalist. In marked contrast, the conflict avoider relies on space, distance, and disengagement for conflict resolution. They often believe—sometimes with considerable accuracy—that the stirring up and repetitious re-shoveling of conflicting emotions is a prolongation of a malignant process already too far underway. The conflict frontalist at their worst is a Pit Bull. The conflict avoider at their worst is an ostrich.

4. Extroversion versus Inversion

The extrovert is someone who desires, reaches out and engages other people as a priority and as a vehicle of attaining well being and happiness; therefore, they seem to "need" lots of people—this is an outgrowth of their orientation.

The introvert, in contrast, has a self-containment orientation. It would be a mistake to assume all introverts are shy and insecure. Introverts often prefer one on one interactions in a large group setting. It takes little imagination in visualizing the challenges implicit in a relationship comprised of an extrovert and an introvert. Which direction do you think you lean towards?

5. Mental versus Physical

This polarity specifically concerns itself with a lifestyle or recreational dimension. Although Freud defined mental health as comprising "good" work and love, he clearly left out "good" play. When couples recreate, how do they do so?

Does one partner prefer stamp collecting, while the other partner prefers sky diving? The mental recreationist seeks pleasures derived from thought, study, mindfulness, and creativity. The physical recreationist seeks more body-associated pleasures derived from sensation, coordination, endurance, and performance.

Recreational possibilities are incredibly broad and diverse. Even partners of highly contrasting polarities can find suitable compromises and choices. For example, a white water rafter can find considerable mental excitement in a game of chess with their significant other.

6. Discomfort with Change versus Comfort with Change

Many factors are at play regarding your feelings about change. At a minimum, they involve your life experience, your goals and dreams, your losses, and your constitution. Change is not one of life's options. It is an inevitable part of your condition and a key component of learning the truth about existence.

Whether it's advisable or not, many people dislike change and format their lives so as to minimize it. Some of the features they emphasize to achieve this are ritual, tradition, routine, habit, regularity, and repetition. These practices can create more predictability in daily life, which makes them feel more comfortable.

Such an approach would seem like soul-death for someone who has comfort with, and a desire for, change. This polarity treats change as the very basis for everything new and vital that life has to offer. These people emphasize the quest for experimentation and new experience in formatting their lives.

When two people in a relationship have significantly opposing feelings about change, there will be problems. The "change-discomfort" person will see their partner as a disrupter, and the "change-comfort" person will see their partner as static and vitality-dead.

7. Rule-Emphatic versus Big Picture Pragmatism

People that are "rule-emphatic" often insist that there is one specific way of doing things and this is simply how things are done. They feel that variation is deviation, and embrace a very black and white, right or wrong approach. Rule-emphatic people in relationships emphasize prescribed, codified living in a moral-intense universe. The means are as important as the results. At their best, these people are reliable, precise, and consistent. At their worst, they are rigid and judgmental.

The "big-picture pragmatist," on the other hand, lives life in the gray shadings, and places more emphasis on results than on the means. These people live in a world where there are many ways of accomplishing the same thing. Overall impressions are often quite sufficient for living and moralizing about behavior is relatively absent. At their best, these people are flexible and results-oriented. At their worst, they are opportunistic and morally opaque.

Some of the most severe relationship conflicts can occur when they involve rule-emphatic versus pragmatic partners. Pragmatic people often feel oppressed, suffocated, and judged by their rule-emphatic partners. On the other hand, a rule-emphatic person may feel a sense of incompleteness, vagueness, and deficiency when they think of their pragmatic partners. These two polarities tend not to mix well in a relationship.

8. Rapid Emotional Resolution versus Slow Emotional Resolution

Emotional resolution as discussed here means the amount of time "needed" to pass from a period of upset back to a recovered "steady state."

Differences in timing for emotional resolutions in relationships is very important because it profoundly affects the collective recovery time for both people in the most tangible ways.

Emotional resolution episodes occur mainly in two different ways in relationships. First, after conflict between both parties and, second, with the personal pain of one of the partners.

In observing two partners after a fight, significant differences between them may be seen, felt, and experienced as to who reintegrates sooner. Yet the actual post-fight interaction of both partners can be sculpted and modified to speed up the recovery time for both. Examples of such actions are amends-making, offering focused listening, corrective actions, empathy enhancement through mirroring, respectful silence, and respectful reaching out through touch. Different rates of emotional resolution may still be apparent despite the most energetic collective efforts of the couple. The best behavior towards the partner who is still hurting is based on tolerance, empathy, and sympathy. People who tend towards more rapid resolution should never state or imply to the other person that they should "get over it," "suck it up," or stop being a "drama queen." This is cruel, insensitive, and inexcusable.

The other instance of emotional resolution episodes occurs with the inner pain and unhappiness of one of the partners. For example, a wife may come home after a bad day at work that was frustrating, disappointing, or painful. It may be clear to the husband and children that she's a bit curt and irritable. Chiding her about her mood by any family member makes a personal issue a family one. It might only be an hour before she feels better or it might take days. Tolerance, sympathy, and offers to listen may enhance resolution, but they may not. Everyone has their own resolution timetable and the best strategy is to respect that.

Sometimes the inner pain of one partner becomes chronic, profound, and relationship-penetrating. Examples of such pain could be major depression, active addiction, chronic rage or chronic anxiety. These illnesses may persist despite the greatest patience and help of the nonsymptomatic partner. In these cases, the suffering partner may have to reach beyond themselves and the relationship and seek professional help. Such a step may prove to be a "win-win" gesture for all parties involved.

9. Life Cycle Experience versus Lack of Life Cycle Experience

In partners with a significant age difference, the superficial observer might be lured and trapped into thinking that because the chronological ages themselves are not congruent, they will present a problem. Such a view misses the point: of equal or greater relevance are the respective life cycle experiences that accompany each person's age that may present a compatibility problem.

For instance, a husband in his sixties who plans on working his entire life need not have a problem with his forty-year-old wife's aspirations of a new full-time job. If he was planning on retiring (his choice, not his age) and traveling the world with his wife, there could be major conflict in the relationship.

The life experience polarity can be an extremely useful tool in measuring what you want to achieve or experience in your lifetime. It will help you and your partner determine what's "been done" and what is "yet to be done." These goals cluster around work, love, and play, and specifically look like:

Work:

- That is satisfying (your work feels good)
- That is financially sound (your work provides for you)

- That is personally meaningful (your work has relevance)
- That is valued by people (you've done your part)

Love:

- That takes the form of good relationship (co-esteeming)
- That gives you joy and provides joy to another (you receive and create good feelings)
- That gives you relevance for the species (support, procreation, etc)

Play:

- That has developed personal inner skills (sports, hobbies, art)
- That has the approval of, and provides pleasure to, others (art, music, competitive sports)
- That has given you a deeper exposure and knowledge of the world (travel).

As the major factors determining life experience, work, love, and play needs have different manifestations throughout the human life cycle. They vary with each individual, family, society, subculture, gender, the epoch we live in, the planetary conditions and countless other factors. For instance, a woman with high procreative needs knows there is a specific window of possibility and opportunity to safely have a child in her lifetime. In contrast, her loving needs span her entire life cycle.

People desiring a long-term relationship absolutely must consider life experience status for themselves and their partner. This involves each person assessing what they have satisfactorily achieved and what they have yet to achieve (but want to) in their lives, and comparing their results to each other.

10. Measured/Inhibited versus Spontaneous/Impulsive

This polarity is especially useful in assessing you and your partners' reactions to new events, situations, and opportunities. A measured/ inhibited person emphasizes thoughtful hesitance when facing new-ness. They often will experience these times cautiously, logically, and will analyze the choice of participating before they do so. In contrast, the spontaneous/impulsive person emphasizes reflexive and feelings-intensive participation when a new situation strikes them as desirable and pleasurable. The former says, "why?"; the latter says, "why not?"

One of my patients revealed an episode of disappointment while vacationing in Cancun with her boyfriend. While enjoying a flawless day on the beach, they were approached by the hotel's recreation direc-tor. He was selling parasail tickets and offered them "instant adventure at a good price." My patient, a long-standing spontaneous/impulsive, leapt at the opportunity to be towed up into the sky and sail over the sapphire sea. "Let's do it," she said, "we'll be like birds." Her boyfriend, who was far more measured and inhibited, asked the director if the activity was safe and what could possibly go wrong. This broke the magic spell for my patient and she grew cross with her partner. She felt frustration with his hesitance. He, in turn, reacted to her with some indignance, and felt she had no right to have a problem "with perfectly reasonable questions." They allowed this conflict between them to sully the next few hours on the sand. What both of these people needed was some tolerance for each others' differences and a spirit of compromise when arriving at a final choice.

The kinds of behaviors a measured/inhibited person engages in lends him or her quite well to new situations when thoughtful, analyti-cal hesitance is necessary. Such times would be when a couple is delib-erating over serious work, business, or financial decisions. When new situations occur in a recreational-play context, spontaneous/impulsive people do a better job of providing the necessary "life in the moment" spirit that gives color and joy to the couple.

When properly managed, these two styles can achieve balance and complement each other throughout the life of the relationship.

17

A Biopsychosocial Model for Couples

Erik Erikson, the famous analyst, is responsible for teaching practitioners to evaluate people in three spheres. This method has come to be known as BioPsychoSocial.

You can evaluate your partner, yourself, and your compatibility by carefully examining these three spheres. You should find this method simple and effective.

Biological

"Bio" (or biological) is every physical factor you can think of. It includes heredity, body type, stature, illness, physical features, and constitutional endowments (i.e., athleticism), to name a few.

Psychological

"Psycho" (or psychological) is every psychological, behavioral or mental factor you can think of. It includes intelligence, psychodynamics, personality, mannerisms, attitudes, and view of the world at a minimum.

Social

"Social" refers to all relevant environmental factors affecting the person. Included in these factors are culture, religion, family influence, and generational influence.

You can do this evaluation in schematic form by following the example below.

BIOLOGICAL	**You**	**Your Partner**
• Aging/Status		
• Body Type/Stature		
• Physicality		
• Hereditary Factors		
• Illnesses/Conditions		
• Racial Specifics (i.e., Sickle cell)		

PSYCHOLOGICAL	**You**	**Your Partner**
• Mental Features-Intelligence		
• Aspirations-Goals-Ambitions		
• Attitudes/Beliefs		
• Personality—Intro/Extro		
• Possible Mental Illness		

SOCIAL	**You**	**Your Partner**
• Culture		
• Religion		
• Social Class/Preference		
• Family Factors		
• Generational Factors		

18

Changing Times, Changing Relationships

The *Housekeeping Monthly* of May 13, 1955, featured "The Good Wife's Guide." It offered the wives of America the following advice regarding the husband's needs after his work day:

- Have dinner ready.

- Prepare yourself.

- Be a little gay and a little more interesting for him.

- Clear away the clutter.

- Catering for his comfort will provide you with immense personal satisfaction.

- Be happy to see him!

- Greet him with a smile.

- Listen to him—remember, his topics of conversation are more important than yours.

- Make the evening his.

- Arrange his pillows and take off his shoes.

- Don't ask him questions about his actions.

- You have no right to question him.

- A good wife always knows her place.

These rigid rules made up the wifely pillars of the Traditional Marriage. Sitting atop the pillars in relative comfort was the husband. The Traditional Marriage that spawned Ozzie and Harriet endorsed a husband-dominating, wife-controlled autocratic relationship where any real partnership or democracy did not exist. Because of the inherent flaws in this form of relationship, the Traditional Marriage was unable to change and evolve. It became a dinosaur. Each constricted and rigid bone that supported it snapped and became a fossil buried in the sands of changing times.

Part of the changing times that are causing the extinction of the Traditional Marriage are social changes. There is less shame about divorce putting an end to a marriage. People are realizing that divorce is a wish to change one's life, and the end of a marriage need not necessarily mean failure. Indeed, divorce may signal an end to suffering and a new beginning. American (and some European) societies are becoming increasingly accepting of newer relationship forms and variations because they may represent a wiser and more effective approach than any tradition has afforded. Marriage and family therapy journals, census, and demographic data document trends into ever-increasing variations of relationship in a growingly accepting social climate. What was possibly scandalous in the fifties may be standard in the new millennium. They are listed below.

Twosomes Living Together

In both the gay and heterosexual worlds, there is a significant tendency to experience living together in the same domicile. No longer constricted by the crushing socioreligious dictum that living together must only follow marriage, live-in couples are at a distinct advantage.

Living together provides information about each person with a detail, richness, and immediacy that other forms of relationship cannot. People rarely make serious commitments without researching it first, and relationships should be at the top of this must-do list.

Unmarried Families

These relationships are simply live-in twosomes with the addition of children. This is where the dynamics of relationships become more than simply one-to-one; with the addition of children, the complexity grows considerably. When a twosome becomes a "family," parent-to-child dynamics come into play, and the couple now embodies parent-to-parent dynamics.

The old stigma of a child being born to an unmarried couple still exists somewhat, and may be the deciding factor for a couple to marry. However, this stigma has lost enough of its potency that unmarried families are increasingly common.

If the unmarried family consists of one biological parent and a non-biological partner, the two-headed issues of step-parenthood and family blending come to the forefront. Although these two issues are beyond the scope of this book, be assured these two factors increase the likelihood and complexity of challenge and conflict significantly for all parties involved.

Remarried Couples/Families

It is likely that the remarried couple/family will become the dominant types of family structure as time goes on. People who divorce will probably go on to get remarried with new partners, hopefully wiser the second or third time around as to what they really need or who they are most compatible with.

With remarriage comes a degree of formalization and obligation. Legal responsibilities increase and involve marital laws that vary state by state. A prenuptial agreement may be entered into by both parties. This defines "legal" eventualities and economic outcomes in the event of divorce. Marital data indicates that a couple with a prenuptial agreement is not more likely to get divorced, although some premarital partners are fearful that this is "starting off on the wrong foot."

For both unmarried couples and unmarried families, the act of marriage often quickens the feelings of all parties involved. In the remarried families, certain features become even more emphasized:

- Step-parenting challenges may increase regarding child-rearing issues, particularly with children in their minority.

- Family blending problems with stepparents may occur.

- Possibilities of name change of children may occur.

- Possibilities of adoption of children if biological ex-spouse is absent or dead.

- Possibilities of shared parental responsibility or joint custody with ex-spouse being affected by remarriage.

- Possibilities of increased problems and expectations between the new parent and ex-spouse.

- Remarriage enhances feelings of finality of prior divorce(s) for all involved.

From these factors, it should be clear that the remarried family faces more challenges than the remarried couple. It is this writer's opinion that remarrying families should proceed very slowly, carefully, and be on the lookout for problems that can grow unwieldly. It might even be wise for the entire "cast of characters" to get some form of premarital family therapy for diagnostic and prophylactic purposes.

Single Parent Family

A parent who divorces is no longer compelled by social shaming or shunning to remarry as soon as possible. Hopefully wiser as a result of divorce, the parent may be emphatic they will not remarry unless the new partner seems like a healthy and compatible prospect as new spouse and stepparent.

Life in a single parent family can be lonely at times. It is particularly important for the parent and child or children not to fuse and become "pals" or "co-consolers" in response to this loneliness. This is important not just for healthy parent-child boundaries. It is also important so that a healthy space remains for a potential new partner. The worst thing a single mother can say to her only or eldest son is, "now you're the man of the house." Children are entitled to a childhood.

It's also important to realize that the longer a single-parent family remains that way, the more it takes on a life of its own, thus creating a self-perpetuating status quo. Older children may be used by a single parent for dialogue, discussion, and decisions that should be reserved only for parents. It's also essential to remember that children do not have voting rights on their single parent's dates, boyfriends, girlfriends, lovers, etc. However, how they feel about their single parent's choice is important and should be discussed if necessary.

Gay and Lesbian Relationship Developments

Many large corporations now acknowledge the legitimacy of gay/lesbian live-in arrangements through domestic partner programs. For instance, health insurance is offered to the domestic partner without necessity for marriage. Gay and lesbian marriages as legal events is an area of growing advocacy and activity on the legislative front.

Adoption of children by gay or lesbian partners is showing increasing activity and advocacy. Adoption of children may not need the same kind of legislative law-making support that marriage does.

America's right wing has cruelly alleged that gay and lesbian relationships, marriages, and child adoptions are sick and unnatural. In my psychotherapy practice, I have seen no differences as to degree of "sickness" when compared to heterosexual couples.

19

Love and Loss in Relationships

In relationships, we often experience love. In life, nothing lasts forever and we experience loss. Loss is the process of suffering we go through when we lose someone we value in our lives.

Loss is inevitable and universal—no matter how hard we avoid it, we all experience loss: nothing is permanent. Therefore, it is true that we shall lose our loved one. For some people, the fear of this loss is so great, they do not permit themselves to love.

Loss is subjective. Each person experiences loss in his or her own unique way. We all experience certain kinds of loss, but the way in which we process it differs tremendously.

Understanding love and loss requires familiarity with the process of loving and personal investment in that love.

Love, and the process of loving, is always changing and growing from one form to another. Love is dynamic and fluid. For love to exist, there must be emotional investment. For emotional investment to exist, there must be safety and gratification. The romantic notion that love is constant, unchanging, and lasts forever is an impossible-to-realize demand.

Emotional investments, loving and bonding involve four important processes:

- Investing outside of oneself into someone or something;
- Introjecting (taking in) the beloved into the self;
- Exposure through time; and

- The emotional mix between two people.

All of these processes can occur at the same time.

The first type of bond is involvement outside of oneself into someone or something. This is illustrated in the expression that one "is really into" someone else. The actual amount of emotional investment in the other person determines the extent of the loss one would feel if the bond were broken and the motivational level regarding preserving the status quo of the bond.

Another bond between people is the introjection of the other into the self. This can be heard most commonly in the phrases "I've got you on my mind…" or "I've got you under my skin." This can be visualized as the other being taken into the heart of the self. This occupancy of the heart takes up space and there is less room for occupancies of similar kinds. This explains the diminished interest one feels in the suitors—competitors of the beloved—when the beloved is occupying the heart of the self.

Another factor affecting emotional investment and bonding is the exposure between two people over time. Simply put, the more exposure between the same two people through the continuum of time, the more likely they are to develop a bond. Each person brings emotional energy fields to every contact. These energy fields can bring forth more knowledge and information about the other person and reveal possible pathways to intimacy, especially when the emotional energy between them has elements of compatibility and complementarity. Exposure through time is an important factor in emotional investment. In most cases, loss of a long-term relationship has a greater impact than loss of a short-term relationship because there has been more time for emotional investment.

Another factor affecting the emotional investment and the potential for closeness is the emotional mix between two people. The emotional mix consists of all the factors affecting the contact between the two people: attitudes, beliefs, values, personalities, constitutions, behavior, personal history, etc. As stated before, a minimum amount of compatibility and complementarity must exist to create the gratification and comfort that fuels the continuation of the bond through time. Even the theory that people pick their opposites as partners to unconsciously fill in their own gaps requires a degree of compatibility. Therapists who work with couples know that compatibility (a gratifying interactive mix) is more helpful to the longevity of a love relationship than romantic or erotic feelings.

Compatibility can be taken too far. The myth of the soulmate is that a perfectly compatible mate exists for everyone, somewhere in the world: one need only find them to ensure a future of unblemished bliss. All people are different and ultimately will want a measure of difference to support selfhood. The only true soulmate you will ever find is yourself.

When you lose a loved one (through death or their leaving), "working" with that loss means initially dealing with their still-present "introject" within you. This consists of deoccupying your heart, mind, and soul. This is a slow, painful process, not an event.

During the early phase of the loss, the "occupied sign" is still hanging. Attempting to bond with another at this time carries an implied hope that the "old tenant" within you will vacate immediately. In reality, the new prospect is taking a number and waiting in line.

The loss of safety and gratification may play a role in your losing your love for someone. Just as you can withdraw money from a failing financial investment, you can withdraw your feelings from an emotional investment if you feel it is genuinely unsafe for you.

The realization of the extent and power of emotional de-investment can be just as painful for the person who has stopped loving as it is for the one who is no longer loved.

In divorce, the comprehension that one feels little or nothing towards the ex-spouse they once loved so much can be extremely sobering. In these situations, don't bog down in the romance-based conclusion that the love was never real or that the relationship was a "failure."

You need to remember that emotional investment and de-investment is dynamic, fluid, and ever-changing. But above all, you need to know at all times that:

For love to flourish, you must nourish.

20

The Loss of a Relationship and Grieving

The normal human emotional reaction to a significant loss is grief. It is also known as mourning or bereavement. Although sadness is the most common symptom, there are many others. In grief, the following transient symptoms may be present:

- Sadness
- Longing
- Crying
- Irritability and Anger
- Raging
- Startle Reactions
- Anxiety
- Restlessness
- Disorders of Sleep
- Disorders of Libido
- Hopelessness
- Remembrances and Flashbacks
- Temporary Phobias
- Forgetfulness

- Preoccupation
- Vengefulness
- Embitterment with Sarcasm

It is important to distinguish grieving from depression. Grieving is always triggered by loss, an explanation of which follows. Depression often is a chronically reoccurring mood disorder triggered by an inner biochemical abnormality. Some symptoms more typical of depression are lack of energy, psychomotor retardation, severe guilt, inability to function, suicidality, and "cognitive scatter."

Types of Loss

All types of loss carry a certain amount of grief. The way you grieve is often different for different types of losses. In order to fully understand grief, it is important to be aware of the different types of loss you experience. Loss may be universal, special, internal, external, chronic, acute, expected, unexpected, mild, moderate, severe, replaceable, or irreplaceable.

If you are suffering from a loss, understanding what type of loss you've experienced can help the healing process.

Universal versus Special Loss

Universal loss occurs at some time in everyone's life, such as the death of, or rejection by, a loved one. It is universal because it is common to everyone.

Special loss (nonuniversal loss) does not happen to everyone. It happens to individuals and can create aggregate groups who have suffered the same type of loss, such as Holocaust survivors or cancer patients. Individuals who suffer from special losses often feel like victims. Therapy or support groups can help them understand the loss, make them realize that they are not alone, and pave the way toward acceptance.

Internal versus External Loss

Internal loss relates to the individual's physical body, such as memory loss or chronic illness. Internal losses are highly subjective in how they affect each individual. The loss of a finger may have much less impact for a psychologist than for a surgeon.

External loss involves other people, things, or situations such as the loss of a job. As people grow older, their ability to deal with an outer loss may diminish. A sixty-five-year-old carpenter will likely find it more difficult to reenter the job market than a thirty-year-old carpenter.

Chronic versus Acute Loss

Chronic loss occurs over a longer period of time and allows you to prepare yourself emotionally and plan for your future. Chronic loss may come in the form of a slowly deteriorating marriage. Retirement is another example of chronic loss that occurs in relationships.

Acute loss is sudden and leaves you little or no time to prepare or plan. An acute loss may be a serious auto accident, an unexpected death, or being fired from a job.

Normal (expected) versus Abnormal (unexpected) Loss

Normal (expected) losses include things you know will happen and generally have more time to prepare for them.

Abnormal (unexpected) losses give you less time for emotional preparation, rearrangement or integration. Abnormal losses may be acute or chronic. A diagnosis of Alzheimer's Disease is unexpected, yet it is a chronic loss that may provide years of gradual decline for the patient and loved ones to adjust to. The sudden death of a previously healthy loved one is an acute unexpected loss.

Mild, Moderate, and Severe Loss

The degree of severity of a loss depends on the level of emotional involvement and the amount of time an individual has invested in it prior to the loss.

Each individual determines the degree of severity of each loss they encounter by the meaning the loss has for them individually and by the socially accepted meaning as well.

Similarly, the same loss may be mild to one individual yet severe to another. Losing twenty dollars is a mild loss to someone with a lot of money but is severe to someone who is struggling to feed a family.

Severe unexpected, acute losses are the most difficult to process, such as accidental death or disabling accidents. These losses are often traumatic and leave an individual emotionally scarred and in a somewhat weakened state in tolerating future losses, especially unexpected losses. They are essentially stuck in the past and function poorly in the present. Often they require some form of help to resume a normal life. People who have experienced a lot of usual expected losses, and have handled them well, are generally better able to cope with future losses.

Replaceable versus Irreplaceable Loss

Finally, loss can be categorized as replaceable or irreplaceable. Again, each individual determines whether a loss is replaceable or not, based upon the nature of the specific loss and the circumstances in which it occurs.

What is Grief Work?

Grief work is the mental, emotional, and spiritual work of the grieving process.

How you do your grief work determines whether growth and healing can occur. Grief work transformation is the process that transforms you from the suffering victim of loss to the more complete person you can eventually become.

Grief work will proceed of its own accord and momentum and will only require TIME…provided nothing interferes with the process.

Roadblocks to Grief Work Transformation

There are potential roadblocks on the grief work journey that can delay your travel. Recognizing these roadblocks will help you clear unnecessary obstacles that stand in the way of your growth. The most common roadblocks are:

- Idealization of what is lost.

- Anger toward what is lost.

- Fear of emotional investment.

- Inability to let go.

- Anxiety over the unknown.

- Fear of being alone.

Idealization of What is Lost. When you idealize what you have lost, you sacrifice your future. For example, a fifty-year-old woman whose husband died exclaimed, "There will never be another like my John. No one will ever be as good as he was, so I'll live my life alone."

While John was unique, the idealization roadblock will destroy her chance of future relationships and the joys associated with sharing intimacy.

Anger Toward What is Lost. Anger is a legitimate emotion; however, this type of generalized anger needs to be examined carefully and eliminated or it stands in the way of your grief work journey. Common phrases like "all men are no good" or "all women can't be trusted" are expressions of anger. Rather than directing the anger toward the individual who has hurt us or let us down, this roadblock generalizes the anger toward all members of a particular sex or group.

Try to identify the source of your anger or you may risk spending your precious future in angry, defensive, lonely withdrawal.

Fear of Emotional Investment. Loss is painful and grief work can be overwhelming. Sometimes the fear of becoming emotionally involved or getting hurt is so compelling that you become isolated. This roadblock prevents interpersonal contact with others and sets an individual apart-like an island surrounded by vast emptiness. Emotional investment is a risk you must be willing to take to move ahead on the grief work journey.

Inability to Let Go. Another roadblock to moving on is unwillingness to leave a situation or relationship that is already over because of one or more of the following reasons:

- Self criticism or regret: If only I just tried harder.

- Pride: People like me don't quit, we try harder.

- Fear of criticism: What will people say?

- Fear of letting go of investment: We put in so much time…how can we give it up after so many years? Let's give it another six months.

Clinging to a hopeless situation only prolongs the grief work journey.

Anxiety over the Unknown. Anxiety over new situations or opportunities—the unknown—keeps you stuck on the grief work journey and prevents you from finding the growth that lies ahead. A housewife contemplating divorce found herself pulling back fearfully. She told her therapist, "The devils I know are better than the devils I don't know."

Fear of Being Alone. Fear of being alone plagues many of us who are contemplating ending a dying relationship. Often we are too afraid to experience solitude because our sense of self is incomplete. We use the other person to "plug up" the gaps. To overcome this roadblock we must be willing to step through those gaps and fill them with our own emotional growth.

The Four Steps of Grief Work Transformation

Recollection

The first step is the active remembrance to that which is being lost or has been lost. This may be accompanied by longing for the pleasures recollected before the loss occurred.

"I wish we could be doing this together."

Review

The second step is to review the loss from your current perspective and see the impact and effect it has had on your current life. You try to speculate about the future implications of the loss.

"I really miss him and now those places seem so empty without him... They'll never feel the same."

Realization

The third step, realization, is the result of the experience gained through the recollection and the array of feelings and ideas derived from the review.

The realization comes from recognizing what parts of the loss are permanent and cannot be negotiated back, and what parts of the loss have opened new possibilities for the future.

"Though I dearly loved her, we turned out to be too different from each other and the relationship needed to end. Perhaps it's time to move on."

Resolution

Resolution is the final conscious step of grief work transformation. It is when you resolve to live life acknowledging the loss. You accept the loss and try to learn from it. Resolution is firmer when it permeates your feelings and ideas and changes your behavior.

"Next time I'll behave in such a way that I'll attract truly available, compatible partners."

Loss and Growth

In order to live in the present, you must be free of the past to the degree that you are sufficiently emptied out enough and free of emotional investment in past relationships, not prejudiced, not preoccupied, and receptive to the influence of the new situation or person. You are never completely disencumbered but you must be adequately free to see each new experience as new. Being available to the newness of a situation creates learning, growth, and further transformation. Loss becomes growth by:

- Freeing up from the past;
- Being available to the unfolding moment;
- Opening up to the newness;
- Learning and further transformation.

About the Author

Mr. Maizler graduated from the University of Miami in 1968, receiving his B.B.A. with honors in Marketing. He earned his M.S.W. with honors at Barry University in 1976, specializing in clinical treatment. He has postgraduate training in psychoanalytic psychotherapy.

Mr. Maizler has been in the private practice of psychotherapy since 1980, and continues working vigorously with individuals, marriages, couples, families, and groups.

He has written and published numerous articles on mental health in such journals as *The Journal of the American Geriatrics Society, Continuing Education for the Family Physician, Journal of Orthopsychiatry,* and *Death Education.* Two of his more recent books on mental health are "Griefwork Transformation" and "The Transformation Handbook."

Mr. Maizler has traveled extensively in Europe, the Mediterranean, and the Tahitian-Hawaiin Pacific. As an angler and writer, his focus has been in the Bahamas, Mexico, and the Caribbean. Mr. Maizler practices in Miami, Florida.

Notes:

Notes:

Notes:

Notes:

Notes:

Notes:

Notes:

Notes:

Notes:

Notes:

0-595-25912-X

Printed in the United States
111594LV00004B/180/A